# Gushing Springs

## LIKE THE WOMAN AT THE WELL, WE CAN FIND FORGIVENESS
## AND FULFILLMENT IN OUR RELATIONSHIP WITH JESUS

## Deborah Lovett

FOREWORD BY

### Donna Partow

ISBN: 1-888237-58-9

Published in the United States by Baxter Press, Friendswood, Texas. Formatting and cover design by Anne McLaughlin, Blue Lake Design, Dickinson, Texas.
Cover photo by T.J. Pfahler.

Printed in Canada

*This book is dedicated to all the thirsty women in the world who feel there just has to be more...*

*In loving memory of my little sister, Bridgett*

*"Jesus answered, 'Everyone who drinks this water will be thirsty again, but whoever drinks the water I give will never be thirsty. The water I give will become a spring of water gushing up inside that person, giving eternal life.'"*

[ JOHN 4:13-14 (NCV) ]

# *Table of Contents*

# Acknowledgements

Above all, I thank my God, through whom my cup runneth over!

Of course, many, many thanks to my cowboy husband, Tim, who disguises himself each day in business attire. I love you darling. You are the best of the best! I could never have done this without your support, your patience, and your love. Let's ride off into the sunset together. You captivate me!

For my precious children: Cristahl and Timmy—thanks for all the times you wanted to talk, and I wanted to type! For being understanding, and all the times you gave me up, out of selflessness to God. May He bless you with a purpose and a passion for Him. Hugs, kisses and all the motherly love I can muster up in Christ. I am so proud of you both.

To my parents, Pat and Jim Carr, thanks for giving birth to me on Easter Sunday, (like you really planned it that way, right?), for giving me a biblical name and for loving me. I love you both so much. And to my sisters Colleen, Vicki and Sherri, I can only imagine what it will be like...

I am deeply indebted to my friends, mentors, disciplers, and prayer warriors who have been faithful to pour into me from the gushing springs of their own love for Jesus for the months or years God asked of them: Nona Anderson, Connie Ange, Diane Bowser, Nancy Caverlee, Jill Cotterman, Emma Fisco, Ruth George, Lucy Grice, Candi Honaker, Sarah Liu, Cheryl Seybold, Pam Walker, Melissa Zimmer and all the devoted women on my prayer team. You are living proof that our wells can be full and overflowing in Christ Jesus!

Thank you to Pat Springle, the editor that made *Gushing Springs* flow!

Of course, to Donna Partow, bestselling author of *Becoming a Vessel God Can Use,* my friend and my writing mentor—thanks for loving and sharing Jesus like you do.

Deepest gratitude to Dr. Kenneth Mahanes, Vice President, Religious Life; Dean, School of Ministry, Palm Beach Atlantic University- who led me to the Lord, baptized me and married me! Bless you!

Thanks to the "flower power" mother daughter duo, Jane and Katie Smith, for their valuable input and love for the Lord. I don't know what I would have done without your encouragement and friendship Jane!

To Delores Metcalf, my domestic angel that prays and cleans while I write and type! You are heaven sent!

Last but not least, thanks to my great grandmother, Edna Frankenburger who wrote the first "Gushing Springs" in 1925 and left the legacy of writing and evangelism to me. Also to my namesake, Aunt Jeanne, who was instrumental in the cover idea. The book you hold in your hands is a union of four generations. My beautiful daughter, Cristahl, is representation of the fourth generation as the cover model!

# Foreword

Nothing compares to the power of a spiritual legacy; no inheritance on earth is worth more than the priceless treasures passed down through the faith of our fathers. Or in Deborah Lovett's case, the faith of her great grandmother. From the moment I first met Deborah, I knew there was something special about her. I sensed that she had tapped into a source of strength, wisdom and joy that few Christians ever discover.

Here on the pages of this book, Deborah has made that source available to the rest of us. She has invested a lifetime quietly cultivating her relationship with her God and has learned to draw deeply from the well of living water. Now, we are the beneficiaries of her devotion to the One she loves with almost reckless abandon.

Gushing Springs doesn't offer any more great ideas concerning how we should live. Honestly, does anyone need any more helpful hints? Isn't there already a never-ending-deluge of Christian books that tell us what we ought to do? What you now hold in your hands offers life itself. You are not about to read a book; you are about to encounter the Living God.

My prayer is that your soul will be refreshed...and that you will return to this spring of encouragement again and again.

*His Vessel,*
*Donna Partow*

# Preface

The hot noonday sun beat down in torturous waves as she made her way through the quiet and lonely streets of Sychar toward the well. She carried more than the burden of her water pots. She also shouldered an oppressive sense of shame, rejection, and guilt as her mind replayed scenes of all the lovers that had turned her away, abused and abandoned her. As hard as she tried, she couldn't forget those images. She heard the stinging memories of people's harsh, condemning words:

"You aren't good enough."

"You're unlovable."

"No one cares about you."

"You'll never amount to anything."

"No one needs you."

"Everyone thinks you're a slut."

"You've messed up your life forever."

She wanted to yell, scream, and wail so someone would hear her cries for help, "Love me, look at me, touch me, just say something to me, p-l-e-a-s-e, anybody!"

The only world she knew was a world of broken promises, hidden agendas, and disappointments. It felt as if her words went nowhere. Her heart was broken in pieces.

Her struggle, though, wasn't against memories. Her real adversary was "the enemy of her soul," who had stolen from her, lied to her, and tried to destroy her life. He had to be overcome. The tables, though, were about to be turned. She was going to be changed from the inside out. The deceiver's plan to destroy her was going to be overwhelmed by God's gracious power and purpose. She was going to stop being a victim. Instead, she was about to become restored and victorious!

As she approached the well, she was subtly interrupted. A stranger with a kind face asked her, "Ma'am, excuse me. Could you give me a drink, please?"

That's how our story begins. It will continue through the winding and turning of conversation, with abrupt detours in dialogue that will leave you hanging on the edge of your seat! This woman's story is like many of us today who are broken, lost, hopeless, despairing, and limping along, following religious ceremony without ever encountering the real intimacy of a relationship with Jesus. But He desires us to drink of the waters of His delight! Drink up—Jesus is coming back, and He wants to prepare His Bride, the church, the people, you and me, His women!

# Before You Begin

It has been my privilege to write this book. It has also been quite a journey. I've found that doing the will of God often conflicts with our worldly desires. Daily pressures, or what our Lord referred to as "the cares of the world," are continuous: the deceitfulness of riches and our lust for things that can steal our hearts. It's becoming harder and harder to be passionate for Christ in our society. Many Christians are lukewarm, withering, no longer drawing life from the Well of Living Water, the Gushing Spring of Jesus Christ.

It's no secret that we are in the end times. Jesus Himself told us to prepare for the evils of the world because life would grow increasingly difficult as the end draws near. At this crucial time in history, we are being called back to our first love, Jesus Christ. We thirst for Him and His return, and we need to meet Him at the Well, on a daily basis in order to be restored, to be transformed into His image, and to share intimacy with Him. Drinking in Christ's love and strength helps us handle this difficult world, and it prepares us for the next! Jesus yearns to come back and meet His Bride, but first He wants to purify her. On your journey to the Well, I pray that you will allow God's Spirit to inundate you with His Power, His purpose, His perspective, and His plentiful love and mercy as you make Him your priority.

This book offers many different ways to journey through it. You can read it like a novel, use it to motivate your walk with Jesus by using it as a devotional with prayer guide, or drink even more deeply by completing the reflections. These questions and exercises at the end of each day's lesson are designed for personal Bible Study or for group discussion. I certainly hope you'll use this book to stimulate wonderful discussions with other women who thirst for Christ!

God's Word needs to be read, prayed, pondered, studied, and applied to our lives. By utilizing all the various functions of *Gushing Springs,* your life will be transformed through God's amazing Holy Spirit. However you choose to use this book, God will honor your efforts to seek Him. No one knows your circumstances better than God does. He knows how much time you need to put into this study in order to receive His greatest peace, blessing, protection, and other tangible benefits. Proverbs 3:4-5 says, "Trust in the Lord with all your heart and lean not on your own understanding; in all your ways acknowledge Him, and He will make your paths straight." Consider these three paths, or ways to journey through the book, and trust God to lead you as you trust in Him!

## *Path #1: Reading the Book as a Novel*

Dear reader, please don't rush your reading. Soak it in and apply what you learn. Enjoy a cup of Chai tea, your favorite latte, or hot apple cider and a delicious chocolate chip scone for me while you're reading! You may want to light a fire, curl up in a comfy chair, sunbathe, go to your favorite spot in the woods, or maybe even sit near a gushing spring! Regardless of the place you choose, your goal is not to just complete the book, but rather to *experience* the intimacy and restoration that comes from your own encounter with Jesus as His Gushing Springs from the fountain of Living Water wash over you. It's best to have one spot rather than searching for a new location each day, and try and set aside the same time each day. Keep distractions to a minimum. Apply your entire heart, soul, body, and mind to the journey—listening and obeying the Holy Spirit's still, small voice along the way. If you choose this route, you probably won't complete the questions at the end of each day. (Drink the Living Water, Deeper Reflections, and Drenched in Prayer.)

## Path #2: Reading to Enhance Devotional Quiet Times and Prayer

If you want to dig a little deeper, study all thirty-five days consecutively with no days off. This way, you'll begin a habit that will fulfill more dreams than you have ever imagined. Allow God's grace to flow over you in abundance!

This book is designed so you can use it in your daily quiet time with God. That way, the study doesn't add anything extra to your already busy schedule! (Unless, of course, you aren't having a daily quiet time. In that case you will find by simply reading the motivational and praying the suggested prayers, you'll also add time and energy to your day.) It's a win/win situation. Our only real defense in the battles we encounter are found in Scripture and in prayer, so at the end of each day's lesson, you'll find Scriptures for reflection (Drink the Living Water) and an opportunity for prayer (Drenched in Prayer). If you've never meditated on Scripture, let me give you a few pointers:

1. Before you begin, sit silently for a minute, asking God to touch your heart and awaken it to an understanding of the truths you are about to read.

2. Read a brief passage slowly. When you are struck by a phrase, note it or mark it. You may even want to look it up in your Bible or a different version and read the few verses before or after to understand the context of the passage.

3. When you finish the passage, focus on the insight or truth that caught your attention. Close your eyes. Ask God to reveal His thoughts to you about a particular word or phrase. You'll have to learn to hear and discern His voice, because at the beginning, you might think you're just hearing your own thoughts.

4. As you perceive what the Spirit is saying to you, consider if it is consistent with Scripture and God's character. If the answer is yes, you've heard from God.

5. Write out (or "journal") God's message to you and how you plan to apply it to your life. Make it short but sweet.

6. Pray for wisdom and help to carry out the revelation.*

Now let me summarize for you: Sit and ask; read and mark; meditate and hear; journal and pray; then; apply. Not bad, huh?

## *Path #3: Deeper Reflections–Study Guide*

Do you remember the movie, Lion King, when Simba looks into a pond and sees the reflection of His father? I enjoy the whole movie, but I adore that part! This is what the "Deeper Reflections" in each lesson are all about. As we look into the reflection of the Gushing Springs of Living Water—as we try on the Word of God—how does it look on us?

In 2 Corinthians 3:18, Paul wrote, "And we, who with unveiled faces all reflect the Lord's glory, are being transformed into his likeness with ever-increasing glory, which comes from the Lord, who is the Spirit." When people look at us, do we reflect our Father? This is the point of the Deeper Reflections. My hope is that you will reflect on the questions in a group format with several other women over the course

---

* Thanks to Christine Wyrtzen, Founder of Daughters of Promise Ministry, for these insights about meditating on Scripture!

of seven to nine weeks. You can write in this book or use a separate notebook. I've found 8 to 12 ladies makes an intimate group, but so does 5 or 6! I've led classes with 4 women, and I've led groups up to 80 women. The key for large gatherings is to break down into smaller groups for prayer and discussion. If you're venturing in your journey without a group, fear not, you're not alone. As I mentioned before, I'm praying for you and God is with you.

This book is "user friendly" because you can actually take it with you to your children's soccer or football games, piano practices or dance classes—you name it—with no need to take your Bible along. Every verse is provided for you. Yes, I spoiled you! But the Scriptures are still the inspired Word of God, whether they come directly off the pages of the Bible or from this book. So I guess you could say this is an "all inclusive journey to the Well!"

I encourage leaders or facilitators of group studies to include props, music, demonstrations, personal stories, dramas, and whatever else the Holy Spirit may lead you to do. Be creative! After all, God is the Creator of the universe. Make your class alive and drenched in the inspiring Spirit of God! Invite your women to start binders and to journal or cut out anything that pertains to what they are learning and share it in class. Oh yes, if you've never led or facilitated a class before, now is the time to begin!

I have one more suggestion to share with you before you begin: No matter which path you are taking, expect God's best for yourself. Look, listen, touch, taste, and smell your way through this book, experiencing all God has for you. Allow Him direct access to your heart, and ask Him daily to awaken your thirst, and then to quench it with His Gushing Springs of Living Water—just like Jesus when He met the Samaritan Woman at the Well many years ago.

# The Place and the Plan

# Games People Play

*The Pharisees heard that Jesus was gaining and baptizing more disciples than John...*

[ John 4:1 ]

irst of all, let me put your fears to rest: this book is not about tennis, bocce ball, golf or any other ball game! People, on the other hand, do play games to try to make sense of their lives. Through the intriguing story of the Woman at the Well, Jesus teaches us about our fears played out through human relationships. But more importantly, Jesus tells us how His love has the power to drive out fear, bringing consolation and restoration through intimacy with Him. Jesus' beloved apostle, John, is known for writing about love, but he also wrote about love's opposite: fear. He connected these two powerful perspectives in his first letter when he wrote, "Perfect love drives out fear" (1 John 4:18). It reminds us that fear and love should not—and in fact, cannot—live in the same space. Thus our story begins...

Many times while reading or listening to the story of the Woman at the Well, authors and speakers start at the fourth verse in the chapter. The first three verses, however, shouldn't be overlooked. They enhance our understanding of this life-changing story. These verses tell us why Jesus was traveling through Samaria. The religious leaders were jealous of Jesus' popularity, so He decided to leave Judea and go to Galilee. His journey took Him through Samaria to people who were despised by the Jews. It was there, in the heat of the mid-day, bright scorching sun, that Jesus encountered our dry, thirsty and spiritually barren, Woman at the Well.

In scene one of the drama, John speaks of the Pharisee's comparisons between Jesus and John the Baptist, which led to their jealousy of Jesus' success and their fears that led to their hatred, condemnation, and murder of Him. Verse one has a "he said, she said" scenario: "The Pharisees *heard* that Jesus..." Oh, you know how it goes: Susie tells Irene a juicy story, then Irene tells it to Dee, changing it dramatically by adding a little detail or inadvertently subtracting a major one. Then, Dee runs to share her "prayer request" with Karen, who promptly tells the first person she runs into at church on Sunday, and then...well, you get the picture! There's a popular song by Gladys Knight and the Pips that says, "Spread the word, I heard it through the grapevine!" The song shows the painful effects of spreading gossip, but Gladys wasn't the first person to reveal the damage inflicted by the verbal grapevine! Unfortunately, people have been practicing this old ritual of jealousy, envy, lying, stealing others' dignity, and gossiping for over 2,000 years. John identified these people in his story as the Pharisees. I can just imagine the stories they made up about our Woman at the

Well, can't you? "I heard Samantha lived with five different men!" Do you hear the parallels? "The Pharisees *heard* ..."

Another tidbit of interest here is that they also played the old game we call "keeping up with the Joneses." The Pharisees were jealous "that Jesus was gaining and baptizing more." Yes, someone was afraid that someone else (not in their circle of friends, not dressed the right way, and not deserving of respect like they were) might get more attention and acclaim. Their competitiveness poisoned their minds and hearts. Why couldn't they just let bygones be bygones? Why couldn't they let each person do their work in peace, without throwing all those ugly stones at others? *I mean we are talking Jesus here, people!* The religious leaders were far more concerned about their own prestige than about the Son of God loving and forgiving people. Like the Pharisees, our eyes can sometimes be blind and our ears can't hear truth. We sometimes aren't able to perceive what God is doing because we are too focused on popularity or position.

The Samaritan Woman wasn't popular. In fact, she had every reason to protect herself from others. She was the object of scorn by her own people, and they, in turn, were the objects of ridicule by the Jews! She was at the bottom of the barrel in terms of respect and admiration. The *Quest Study Bible* says women in that day sometimes married just to be able to eat. The Samaritan Woman had been hurt so many times that she didn't trust people, and she may very well have been quite cynical too.

At times I can be just like her, distrusting others because I'm not sure if they'll treat me with respect. Instead of being open to them, I immediately shut them out. Guilty until proven innocent, right? Although my intention is not to throw stones, I also know how it feels when the stones come flying, don't you? I imagine our Samaritan

Woman had seen a few flung in her direction for not measuring up with the Joneses in Samaria and failing to meet the Pharisees' standard of perfection. Being a divorcee, after all, isn't exactly the model of purity they would want their own daughters to follow. Jealousy fuels competition and condemnation, and it's very destructive, hurting everyone in its path.

We expect the games of comparison to be found in our society, but unfortunately, we also find them in our own church families. Yes, women can be famous for splitting hairs, manipulation, and jealousy. I've heard it excused in many ways, but it all really boils down to pride. Let's be careful not to forget our battle is not against flesh and blood. The comparisons, rationalizations, and raw envy that can control our minds are rooted in the same fears that the Pharisees experienced when they noticed Jesus' popularity. These are the games people play. There's nothing new under the sun. These games end in divorce, addictions, betrayal, bitterness, depression, financial traps, as well as death.

The beginning of the fourth chapter of John's gospel is just one little verse, but it contains a big lesson. This lesson about the Woman at the Well speaks to our hearts today. We can turn from our pitiful, destructive games and ask God to fill us with His love, wisdom, and strength. *Jesus is coming back, and we need to get the Bride of Christ ready! It's time to advance the Kingdom, rather than continuing to retreat!* For today, let's remember that the bondage of fear can cause people to play games as they try to fill up the empty well in their hearts with approval, affirmation, position, power, possessions, and yes, even love.

Leaders already in positions of power can clog the flow of God's love and encouragement due to their jealousy and fear. God's Word stands as our plumb line of truth and purity, and where the Spirit of Lord reigns, there is freedom from these fears. *We can have faith in what Jesus Christ has done for us through His love shown for us on the cross, which frees us from fear today.*

Perfect love truly does drive out fear. Let Him love you perfectly at the Well today. And then, while you soak up His care and strength, love others the same way.

## Drink the Living Water

"But encourage one another daily, as long as it is called today, so that none of you may be hardened by sin's deceitfulness." [Hebrews 3:13]

"For God does not show favoritism." [Romans 2:11]

"Those who belong to Christ Jesus have crucified the sinful nature with its passions and desires. Since we live by the Spirit, let us keep in step with the Spirit. Let us not become conceited, provoking and envying each other." [Galatians 5:24-26]

## Deeper Reflections

Think about these questions:

— In the last two days, have you been involved in gossip? If you have, what did you actually hope to accomplish by talking about that person?

— Have you tried to control things to have your own way due to fear or envy? If so, explain what you did and why you did it.

— Do you spend more time examining others prestige and popularity than examining the love God has poured out on you? Explain your answer.

— Do you play other games, such as the "pity-party," "let's argue," "let's pretend," or "let's be silent" game? If so, how do these affect your thoughts, your behavior, and your relationships? What fears are causing you to play these games?

— Who are you actively seeking to encourage today that may be in the grip of fear?

— What are some truths about your identity as a beloved child of God that you need to focus on today?

## Drenched in Prayer

*Lord, thank you for Your example to me. Show me where I fall short today, and remind me that Your love is unconditional. Help me to not let pride lead the way, but to remember Your perfect love drives out fearful unbelief in my life. I invite You today to come into my life and show me where I play games. Lord, transform my heart. I want to be so in love with You that my mind is totally occupied continually with Your greatness and my words are filled with praise and thankfulness. Help me walk in faith, not fear, and in love, not lies. Meet me at the Well right now. Amen.*

Take time to sit and listen for God and respond to Him.

# The Facts

*...although in fact it was not Jesus who baptized, but His disciples.*

[ John 4:2 ]

The truth always comes out. The Pharisees thought Jesus had been baptizing followers, "although in *fact* it *was not* Jesus"! This is the end of the "he said, she said" game in the first verse. I bet those control freaks that always had to get their own way sure were having a hissy fit over this one! "What?" I can almost hear them saying, "You mean I've spread that information about Jesus among my closest friends, and now I find out it's not true after all?" Gulp, I think foot-in-mouth syndrome just set in. Now they had a choice: They could go hide in the corner, or they could make up another deliciously juicy lie—this time bigger and better! That would take the attention off them and put it back on someone else.

This is called the "pass the blame and then complain" game. Some play it really well, and they never stop to think their complaints and accusations might be wrong. Never in a million years! We can complain and be drained or praise and be raised—that's a fact!

The fact remains, that the facts are the facts are the facts, and that's a fact. But in today's society, it's not that simple, is it? *People lie about the facts; some lawyers change the facts; the news media embellishes the facts; many citizens are misled about the facts.* Isn't it amazing how two people can see the same thing happening, and yet they come up with two entirely different descriptions of the event? Take for instance, the stay-at-home mom who drinks to ease her pain from living with an emotionally abusive husband. The neighbors may only see the drunken wife and are quick to pass judgment on such horrendous behavior, while the husband charms their socks off. But a family member of the woman may see a hurting mom stuck in a situation that looks hopeless. Most of us have seen circumstances such as this. The facts present themselves differently, depending on where you're standing, whose eyes are doing the seeing, and whose heart is doing the listening.

So what's the answer? We need to see what God sees and hear what God says. We need to consider the wisdom of God, which is called "spiritual discernment." Because the Holy Spirit takes up residence inside Christians, we can always look to Him for guidance, instruction, and insight on any matter. All it requires is a choice to ask and listen. (That's the hard part!) God always presents the truth to us in His Word. When we believe God's Word over man's word, we get the truth, pure and simple.

In verse two, we remember that God wants all people to come to repentance and be baptized. The issue wasn't the person who baptized or how many were baptized.

Today, many people compare the number of people who attend different churches, but that's not the issue. God's main agenda is always the transformation of people's hearts through repentance, forgiveness, love, and grace. That was a fact 2000 years ago, it's a fact now, and it's a fact that will never change. Love transcends all. In 1 Corinthians 13:3, Paul said, "If I give all I possess to the poor and surrender my body to the flames, but have not love, I gain nothing." God is on mission to heal a hurting world. Petty comparisons only cloud our minds and hearts. God is love, and whoever dwells in Him dwells in love. Satan has tricked us into making the numbers game a top priority. The desire for numbers may have spawned mega-churches, but size really doesn't matter. We bear fruit by our love, and without love, the numbers mean nothing. Numbers aren't important, but people are. God doesn't want a single soul to perish (2 Peter 3:9). He wants every human on the planet to experience His redeeming love. That is a huge number! His love is overwhelming, His vision is huge, and His heart is full of compassion. With God anything is possible!

To be honest, we all have a tendency to go down the dark paths of constructing our own version of reality. For example, if someone is abusive to you or breaks a promise, you might believe, "I'm not worthy of being treated right or having a promise to me kept." Or perhaps you have even gone to the opposite extreme and lashed out in bitterness: "That lying bum isn't worth anything, that slug!" But we are all made in God's image. We are tarnished by sin, but Jesus turns no one away from His grace. Prejudice isn't in His vocabulary, which is precisely why He chose to go through the alien land of Samaria to meet our *Well Water Woman*. (Say that, five times real fast!)

We need to examine the "facts" we so easily accept! We need to compare them to the facts God gives to us as His daughters. It's a lesson I've been working on my whole life. With time, experience, and wisdom, it gets easier to discern fact from fiction, but I'm still aware of my tendency to allow what may seem to be the facts to lead me in a downward cycle of unbelief and self-condemnation. That spiral ends in the belief that everything that goes wrong is "all my fault." It's a cycle that has been difficult to stop and reverse, but when I remember Jesus and His unconditional love, I'm encouraged. Does this ring a bell for you, too?

We need to be aware of the lies that come from people and the enemy of our souls, and we need to give more focus and energy in order to develop an accurate perception of our holy, loving, and powerful God!

A warning to us is written in between the lines of today's lesson: Beware of people who use one verse of Scripture as the basis for an entire theology. *Even the enemy knows Scripture. Be alert and know God for yourself so you can discern the truth for yourself.*

## Drink the Living Water

"Understanding is a fountain of life to those who have it, but folly brings punishment to fools." [Proverbs 16:22]

"But when he, the Spirit of truth, comes, he will guide you into all truth. He will not speak on his own; he will speak only what he hears, and he will tell you what is yet to come." [John 16:13]

"...the reality, however, is found in Christ." [Colossians 2:17]

## *Deeper Reflections*

— Do you have a need for God's truth in your life? How regularly and how intently are you reading His Word?

— Do you constantly blame others for the circumstances in your own life? What do you hope to accomplish by blaming them?

— Is there a recurring sin in your life that is blocking your relationship with Christ? If so, look at 1John 1:9 and confess that sin. What would true repentance look like in your life?

— Are you prepared to believe God's Word and apply it, regardless of what others think? Explain your answer.

— Is there something you are confused about today? Are you willing to pray and ask God to help you discern the truth of your situation? Will you seek His Word for truth? What will be the benefits of gaining God's perspective on your confusing situation?

# Drenched in Prayer

*Jesus, fill me with the Living Water of Your character. You re-main the same, Your Word remains the same, and Your love remains the same no matter how everything around me may change. Although I need to make changes, I can't change without the assurance of Your unchanging character. Help me to see truth, hear truth, and act accordingly, not reacting to lies meant to steal my peace and joy. Thank You for illuminating my way to the Well today. Amen.*

# Learned and Left

*When the Lord learned of this, He left Judea and went back once more to Galilee.*

[ John 4:3 ]

"Learned" and "left" arc the significant words in today's lesson. When you think about it, these words seem strange when they are used to describe Jesus. How does the Son of God learn anything? Does He look it up in a religious book or encyclopedia? Or go ask the Pharisees? (I don't think so!) Since He was the Son of God, He had some pretty special connections, so I bet if He wanted, He could just go straight to the top!

If you're at all like me, you may have had seasons in your life when you tended to use others' opinions, rather than God, as your plumb line for advice. One is fickle; the other is infinite. When my earthly father talks to me, I listen, (although he may question that statement!) but I really pay attention to my heavenly Father! The Pharisees could have eliminated a lot of grief in their lives if they had just asked Jesus what was going on. *Honesty, openness and authenticity go a long way in eliminating games in relationships.* In this verse, Jesus is telling us to not rely exclusively on what we hear from others, but at least sometimes, to learn for ourselves.

Speaking of learning, did you know that the word "disciple" actually means learner? We are first and foremost disciples of Jesus Christ. Yes, we learn from our church leaders, but our first allegiance is to Christ. We can almost always assume our pastors, spiritual directors, and bible study teachers have the best intentions, but at times even they can mislead us. Always check what you hear against the Word of God, especially when your spirit senses that something you hear may not be quite right. Jesus knew the truth, because Jesus was Truth in person—and He still is today! When we are His disciples, it's our responsibility to keep learning through Bible reading, prayer, studies, and most importantly, through our personal relationship with Him by visiting Him at the Well daily. A lack of learning and growing results in an emptiness deep down inside.

At this time in John's gospel, Jesus was just beginning His ministry. At this crucial point, He *left* Judea rather than stay and confront the opposition. Beth Moore, a favorite bible teacher of mine, advises us, "Never stay and argue with a Pharisee." I couldn't agree more. A Pharisee is known as one who separates, rather than unifies. I'm so sorry for the times I have acted like a Pharisee, but I'm even more sorry for the times I stayed to argue with one. That's just wasting time.

What do we do when we hear that others are spreading rumors about us? Well, let's see. First, we probably feel hurt, then we get angry, then we may spend all night trying to figure it out in our pretty little heads, and then we get revenge! Or maybe, just maybe, you're the type, the rarity, and the jewel in the rough, who forgives and moves on. What? Is that possible? Yes, our Scripture for today says, "He left Judea." In the same way, you and I can forgive an offense and walk away without demanding change, retribution, or vindication. That's a difficult task, *especially in our culture that is known for its victim-mentality*—but it's possible if we follow Jesus.

At this particular moment, Jesus chose not to confront the Pharisees. A time would come when He would stand up boldly to them, but this was not that moment. As Kenny Rogers used to sing, "You gotta know when to hold 'em, and know when to fold 'em. Know when to walk away, know when to run!" Jesus simply wasn't concerned that the Pharisees misunderstood His role in the baptism of believers. He was far more interested in hearts being transformed by His love and power. He still is. He saw no need to defend Himself or explain His role. He kept His eyes focused on pleasing His Father and talking to people— even outcasts! —about His love.

If the Pharisees had been open to Christ instead of jealous of His popularity, perhaps Jesus would have stayed longer in Judea. We'll never know. Jesus responded to the fact of their hardened hearts, and He looked for people who would respond to His love. He knew their hearts better than they knew themselves. But too often, we're like the Pharisees. Oh, how long it takes us to choose to leave and forgive! We'd rather stay, prove ourselves, and protect our reputations. Those efforts block forgiveness and inhibit our freedom. When we hang on to our anger, then bitterness and resentment grow in our hearts. (Sorry if I pinched a nerve here, but this is important!) Bitterness sours our attitudes and ruins every relationship. It's a plague in our lives.

I wonder how many of us need to leave something behind? We may not leave physically and geographically, and we certainly won't leave all of our relationships. But we may need to leave a negative attitude, a destructive habit, or haunting thoughts behind. But not every difficulty is something we should leave. In some cases, God calls us to persevere through our struggles instead of running away. How do we know the difference? Time at the Well with Jesus does wonders to give us wisdom and understanding. It helps us *learn*. And yes, sometimes we have to go back to where we started to find our Father's will once again. Or we may think we know what God wants us to do, but we aren't quite sure. In that case, we need to go back and receive confirmation. Think, pray, and pay attention. If you don't *prepare*, you will probably have to *repair* later (believe me on this)! Proceed slowly, watching and trusting God to lead you. My good friend, Donna Partow, best selling author of *Becoming a Vessel God Can Use* says, "God's will is never a crisis!" To which I say, "Amen to that sister!"

Remarkably, within the first three power-packed verses of John Chapter Four, Jesus' disciples were already trained and out on the battlefield. The Pharisees, however, were left behind with their own agenda. Isn't this what happens? Some people focus on the wrong things and are left behind, but the obedient ones are blessed as they learn about Jesus. They leave behind their worldly cares and drink deeply from the fountain of Living Water!

## *Drink the Living Water*

"Throw off everything that hinders and the sin that so easily entangles, and let us run with perseverance the race marked out for us." [Hebrews 12:1]

"I have learned to be content whatever the circumstances." [Philippians 4:11]

"My people are destroyed from lack of knowledge." [Hosea 4:6]

"I urge you brothers, to watch out for those who cause divisions and put obstacles in your way that are contrary to the teaching you have learned. Keep away from them. For such people are not serving our Lord Christ, but their own appetites. By smooth talk and flattery they deceive the minds of naïve people." [Romans 16:17-18]

"Therefore go and make disciples of all nations, baptizing them in the name of the Father and of the Son and of the Holy Spirit, and teaching them to obey everything I have commanded you." [Matthew 28:19: ]

## Deeper Reflections

— In what ways have you seen the effects of jealousy and bitterness in other's lives? Have you seen those effects in your own life? If so, how have you resolved that problem?

— Is there an area of your life today that you feel God's Holy Spirit nudging you to leave it behind? Or is there a personal situation that you have no control over and just need to turn your focus to God rather than to another person? Explain your answer.

# Drenched in Prayer

*God grant me the serenity to accept the things I cannot change, and the courage to change the things I can, and the wisdom to know the difference. Help me not to be offended, remembering all that You went through for me on the cross as I leave behind the things of earth that I may fall prey to. May thy Kingdom come and thy will be done in my life today, as well as those around me. Amen.*

# Had to Go

*Now He had to go through Samaria.*

[ John 4:4 ]

Have you ever run out of gas because you had to be somewhere at a certain time, and you were too rushed to stop? Or have you listened to a little one screaming, "Mommy I have to go potty, now!" There are certain things in life that just have to be done. For Jesus this was one of those unchangeable journeys that just *had* to be done. He *had* to go through Samaria. And boy, I'm glad He did! His intriguing conversation with one Woman at the Well in Samaria has had a far -reaching effect on all of us. The interesting thing is that most Jews would have gone *around* Samaria, trying to avoid it all costs, but not our Jesus. He was determined to go there to show us how He loves the unlovable. It was something He had to do.

Have you ever heard that there is a way you have to go? Have you ever heard a voice behind you saying, "This is the way, walk in it"? (Isaiah 30:21)

Jesus had to go *through* Samaria, not around it, over it, under it, but through it. Sometimes we, too, have to go through things rather than just ignore them, deny them, wish them away, or turn elsewhere. I must admit, I've been a pro at running away from things most of my life. I wish I could have blocked out the fact that my sister took her own life at the young age of forty, but instead, my family and I had to go through it. Isaiah 43:2 says: "When you pass through the waters, they will not sweep over you." Sometimes God allows us an easy road, but sometimes He takes us through life's most turbulent and deepest waters. The Father wanted to heal my grief, and He did when I chose to go through it with Him rather than denying and repressing the natural mourning process.

There are certain things we should do, others we need to do, and some that just happen due to the fact we live in a fallen world. But our faithful Father promises to lead, guide, comfort, and protect us through our entire faith journey as we put our trust in Him. Notice I said, "journey." Jesus' trip to the well was a journey, and so was His unbearable trip to the cross at Calvary. Similarly, our lives are not an event, but a journey to be embraced. Sadly, many women are living "thirsty lives," not realizing that their souls are tired from the journey and they are dying for the Gushing Springs of Living Water. We need to acknowledge and embrace our thirst for Jesus. *For our thirst to be quenched, we need to focus on the journey, not only on the destination.*

Our salvation and eternity with Jesus are secured through our acceptance of His sacrifice for our sins, yet our souls can live unsatisfied if we only dip from the Well once in a great while. A rich, rewarding relationship with Jesus takes more than an occasional taste of Living Waters. We need to drink deeply and often.

Our faith journey can be a difficult thing, requiring that we say "no" to our selfish desires and instead submit to the Holy Spirit. That's exactly the example Jesus gave us in His own life on earth. Through good times and bad, Jesus always did what pleased the Father. In this case, Jesus submitted…

- for a woman
- for a purpose
- for a freedom
- for a city
- for a lesson
- for His disciples
- for obedience
- for His Father
- for a love
- for us!

Jesus walked this path to an alien land because He was motivated by His love for the people in Samaria. But why that place? Samaria was a bi-racial culture, a Jewish/foreign mix. The orthodox Jews looked down their noses on Samaritans. (That's a nice way of saying the Jews were stuck-up, conceited, and self-righteous!) In fact, they would take a much longer route to get to their destination in order to bypass Samaria. Jesus was a Jew. He could have bypassed Samaria, but He knew it was the will of the Father for Him to go *through* that area. His obedience brought blessing beyond words. Similarly, our own lives will only be effective when we are responsive to God's instructions, commands, mercy, and love.

Henry Blackaby, the author of *Experiencing God,* says, "You can't stay where you are and go with God." Jesus didn't take the road most traveled. When everyone else would have gone around Samaria, He went through it. There's a lesson for us here. Sometimes we have to leave something that is hindering our walk with God, and sometimes, like this verse, we have to go through a difficult situation for our faith to grow stronger. Either way, God goes with us. Jesus celebrated His first unopposed success in ministry by going through Samaria. He experienced the blessing of being obedient.

We all have times when "the call" of God's purpose isn't pleasant—and perhaps even severely trying at times. We may be called to endure a difficult trial or extreme suffering. Whatever it is that we endure, it's nothing like the pain Jesus faced on the cross. Think of where He went for us so that we could spend eternity with Him—but don't forget the journey that took Him there.

Not only did Jesus choose to go through Samaria for the Woman at the Well, but He also chose to go to the cross for you and me. Our love for Him today compels our spirits to identify His voice when He speaks to us and urges us to connect with Him through prayer. Our thought processes lead to actions, and actions lead to habits. I want to develop the habit of practicing His presence today. The Kingdom of God is within me.

Let's submit to the journey God has for each of us and go through the waters that make faith grow. Instead of going around difficulties, let's meet Jesus even in a troubled, alien land at the Well that Gushes Springs of Living Water. He died to satisfy our thirst so abundantly! Just look at the blessings that flowed from the Woman at the Well! And always remember, "He" is the blessing!

## *Drink the Living Water*

"Then I heard the voice of the Lord saying, 'Whom shall I send? And who will go for us?' And I said, 'Here am I. Send me!'" [Isaiah 6:8]

"But blessed is the man who trusts in the Lord, whose confidence is in Him. He will be like a tree planted by the water that sends out its roots by the stream. It does not fear when heat comes; its leaves are always green. It has no worries in a year of drought and never fails to bear fruit." [Jeremiah 17:7 -8]

"And the God of all grace, who called you to his eternal glory in Christ, after you have suffered a little while, will himself restore you and make you strong." [1 Peter 5:10]

## *Deeper Reflections*

— What situations are you experiencing that seem like they take you to a strange, alien land?

— Should you go around them, or should you walk through them? Explain your answer.

— How would the life of the Woman at the Well been different if Jesus hadn't gone through that town?

— How might Jesus meet you in your own Samaria to meet your needs like He met the Woman at the Well?

## Drenched in Prayer

*Father, my heartaches in pain for some of the trials and hardships I go through. Please let me face them in a godly manner, remembering all that You went through, and Your faithfulness. May my faith be refined in the fires, and may my character burn brightly for You as well. In my sufferings, help me to be like Jesus. Use Your Word to show me the way I should go. Thank You for Your grace and Your Holy Spirit. Amen.*

*Authors note: Suicide is a permanent solution to a temporary problem. If you are having despairing thoughts of suicide please contact the suicide prevention center nearest you. They can help. They do care. God loves you.

# God Is a Giver

*So He came to a town in Samaria called Sychar, near the plot of ground Jacob had given to his son Joseph.* [ John 4:5 ]

E ven before God created the universe, He had a plan for the plot of ground Jacob gave his son, Joseph. I imagine Jacob had no idea of the coming and goings that this plot of land would experience! Sometimes things happen, and we have no idea why. God's ways and His thoughts are higher than ours. (Isaiah 5:9) Today, let's remember that He knows far more than we do about every aspect of our lives.

When God created the land around Jacob's well, He made more than just a plot of ground to house stagnant rainwater for watering animals. He gave food and drink, a place for people to meet and greet, and a legacy of grace and forgiveness to pass down through generations to us. This land became the scene of the drama in John Chapter Four.

God gave this land to Jacob, and Jacob gave it to Joseph. God is a giver, hoping we will receive His grace and love! Think about all that God has given over the years; He gave the Israelites the Promised Land, flowing with milk and honey; He gave Solomon great wisdom; He gave David a heart like His; He gave Deborah great victory in battle (I love that one!); He gave Rebekah her husband Isaac by a well; He gave Rachel her husband Jacob by a well; He gave Mary a virgin birth; and He gave the Samaritan Woman a new reputation by Jacob's well! *Most importantly, God gave us Jesus, the cup of the new and living testament that was poured out for our sins.*

Jesus is the best gift ever, for God is the giver of all good and perfect gifts. God's economy is not the same as our economy. He never goes into recession, and the entire universe is His possession. Not only did God create all that we hear, see, touch, taste, and feel each day, but He entrusts part of it to us as we can handle it according to His purposes. I say, "God is the owner. We are merely the managers of what He gives us."

I've always told my husband he should have bought stock in the Christian bookstores before I began reading! Think of all the authors you love to read. God gave them the ability to communicate His heart. I often think of the women God has sent to disciple or mentor me through the years. What did God give them? Wisdom to deal with me, and plenty of patience and insight. I am indebted to each of them!

What has God given you today? It may be financial wealth, a special talent for music, cooking, hospitality, or something else. Maybe He wants you to use your home to invite someone over for a life changing conversation, like Jesus had with the Samaritan Woman. Maybe He wants you to use your talent in writing to inspire others to grow closer to Him. Maybe He has given you the gift of teaching so you can share a Bible study with your neighbors. Maybe He has given you mercy or encouragement and wants you to show His love to the homeless, feed the hungry, or give a child a home. Maybe He has given you trials beyond belief to demonstrate your trust in Him. I don't know. But God expects us to use what He gives us for His plan and His purpose, all to His great glory! We are not to waste His gifts. We are invited to take from His supply and give from ours!

Oh, how great is His love that He includes us in His plan to redeem a lost and hurting world! Don't confuse the gift and the Giver. John 3:16 "For God so loved the world that He gave His one and only Son, that whoever believes in Him shall not perish but have eternal life." Let's live a life of purpose, shall we?

## Drink the Living Water

"Every good and perfect gift is from above, coming down from the Father of the heavenly lights, who does not change like shifting shadows." [James 1:17]

"Whoever has will be given more, and he will have an abundance. Whoever does not have, even what he has will be taken from him." [Matthew 13:12]

"Until I come, devote yourself to the public reading of Scripture, to preaching and to teaching. Do not neglect your gift…" [1 Timothy 4:13-14]

"'For I know the plans I have for you,' declares the Lord, 'plans to prosper you and not to harm you, plans to give you hope and a future. Then you will call upon me and come and pray to me, and I will listen to you. You will seek me and find me when you seek me with all your heart. I will be found by you,' declares the Lord, 'and bring you back from captivity.'" [Jeremiah 29:11-14]

## *Deeper Reflections*

— Make a list of the gifts God has given you. Think about meaningful relationships, possessions, wonderful experiences, etc. Take some time to thank him for these gifts.


— What do others say your talents are? What do you say they are?


— What assignment has God given you to accomplish for Him today? Have you asked the Giver what He wants you to do? How will you use your talents to accomplish it? How you can better serve Him?


— Pray for a plan or purpose from God for your life today.

## Drenched in Prayer

*Almighty God, You knew me before You created the land for Jacob's well, and You know the purpose and the plans You have for me. They far outweigh anything I can fathom! Lead me in the paths of Your righteousness, and help me to persevere in seeking Your destiny for me. May I always put You first, knowing that You are the Rock, the foundation of all. May Your Gushing Springs drench me today with purpose and passion as You speak to my heart about my gifts and talents. May I use all I have to bring You the glory You deserve. Amen.*

# The Woman
# and the Well

# *Well Rest*

*Jacob's well was there and Jesus, tired as He was from the journey, sat down by the well. It was about the sixth hour.* [ John 4:6 ]

It was Jesus' time to *rest* because He was tired from the journey. That's so simple and yet so difficult for us to do. Listen up ladies: If we get tired, we should follow Jesus' model and rest. We not only have His permission; we have His example!

Jesus, as perfect and sinless as He was, *got tired.* Not a tired from being sick or stressed out. Not a tired from carrying resentments and bitterness around for so long that His spirit was worn out. His weariness was a plain, old tired from walking and talking, from the daily stuff of life. I can relate, can't you? Normal life can be wearisome even *without* all the extra trials and burdens we so often carry. Our culture yells to us: "Take the kids! Do the laundry! Fertilize your yard! Fix a gourmet meal! Heal that hurt! Exercise more! Eat less! Wear this! Try that!" Ugh. Dishes, groceries, bills, work, sick kids, tired husbands, and high-maintenance families can about put a girl in the funny farm, and that's without deaths, addictions, divorces, abuses, cancers, hurricanes, earthquakes, and terrorist attacks. (Sometimes I think I have no other choice but the funny farm!)

So what did Jesus do when He got tired? He sat down by the well. He wanted to take a little afternoon siesta and get a long cool drink of water to quench His real-life physical thirst. And which well did He choose to sit by? None other than the well of Jacob. This well wasn't one of those spring-fed wells that we pay good money to get a bottle from. (Have you seen the fancy square bottles with the flowers on them? What will they think of next?) No, this was just a plain old rainwater well. For you history buffs: Jacob's well is currently about 135 feet deep, and water can be located about 85 feet down. In Jesus' day and today, it's the place in that area to get water. We all know that water is not a luxury but a necessity. But then again, so is rest.

It wasn't a coincidence that Jesus came at the sixth hour. In our language, that's noon. It was extremely hot at that hour. Most women came to draw water in the cooler parts of the day, the early morning and early evening. The Samaritan Woman, however, came at the hottest time of the day. Jesus met her when she thought she was alone and safe from the ridicule of others—at a lonely point of despair and desperation. It's just like Jesus to meet her at a well that holds stagnant well water when He Himself is the Gushing Spring of Living Water! Alone at the well with Jesus. AHHHhhhh! Savor the moment, taste the refreshment found in Jesus! Just think of it!

When is the last time you were tired, and took a little time for some ice-cold lemonade with your children or grandchildren? Or when is the last time you said to a weary soul, "Let's sit down together and just chat"? Or when is the last time you took the time to prioritize your to-do list and schedule time for rest instead of running fifteen errands in fourteen minutes flat? (On some days I can do them in thirteen!)

Busyness rules our lives, which in turn dehydrates our souls. Is your soul dehydrated? Take the ABC test: A is for angry or addicted, B is for bored or bitter, and C is for controlling or confused. Are any of those true for you today?

There's a difference between worldly rest and well rest. We try everything to fill our need for rest with anything and everything else. We leaf through magazines, go to the movies, turn on the car radio, or go shopping. The list goes on and on of the things we do, and we call it "resting." The enemy of our souls lies to us by convincing us that we are really resting when we aren't. Our bodies may even be still, but our minds and hearts are still racing. Rather than allowing ourselves the necessity of genuine rest, we think of it as a luxury.

Today, rest is something we must make an intentional choice to do. *Remember that to make no choice at all is to make an unintentional choice to live in a state of unrest!* And rest is also a habit we learn to develop. What? Learn to rest? You've got to be kidding! In the book of Philippians, we read that Paul had to *learn* to be content, and we have to *learn* to rest. Here is my simplified idea of rest: It involves your body, soul (your mind, will, and emotions), and your spirit:

First, your body: choose to sit still. Pick a comfy couch, cuddly blanket or cozy chair, in a special spot, room, woods, or your garden.

Second, your soul: empty your mind. (That means no television or books.) Seek solitude!

Third, your spirit—be still and know that He is God, (Practice His presence.)

God promises to give us rest when we come to Him and let go of our cares. Isn't that wonderful? One stipulation though, we must come believing!

REST stands for:

- Replenished with the Living Water,
- Emptied of self,
- Sitting at the feet of Jesus, and
- Trusting in God.

I suggest you start by *trusting* Jesus will meet you at the Well. Then take a seat in faith knowing He is *sitting* with you. Next, *empty* yourself of selfish desires, submitting to Him. Lastly, ask Him to give you that Living Water that *replenishes* your body, soul, and spirit. Why start at the end with the "T" and work forward to the "R"? Because in our busy, hurried world, it's "backward" for us to rest, so we have to make the choice. And it starts by trusting that when you take some time to seek God, He'll bless your time and give you enough time for all the necessary things in your day.

God has given us time for every activity under the sun. And now, today, it's your time to *rest*. What will you choose today?

## Drink the Living Water

"There remains, then, a Sabbath-rest for the people of God; for anyone who enters God's rest also rests from his own work, just as God did from his. Let us, therefore, make every effort to enter that rest, so that no one will fall by following their example of disobedience." [Hebrews 4:9-11]

"Come to me, all you who are weary and burdened, and I will give you rest. Take my yoke upon you and learn from me, for I am gentle and humble in heart, and you will find rest for your souls. For my yoke is easy and my burden is light." [Matthew 11:28-30]

"This then is how we know that we belong to the truth, and how we set our hearts at rest in His presence whenever our hearts condemn us. For God is greater than our hearts, and He knows everything." [1 John 3:19]

## *Deeper Reflections*

— On as scale of 0 (not at all) to 10 (totally), are you a driven person? Has the enemy deceived you into believing that you simply *must* do something, go somewhere, or perform some task every moment of the day?

— Will you come today to the Well to rest because you love Jesus, trusting that He promises what you long for today? What thoughts or attitudes might hinder this rest?

— Have you ever really thought about your own thirst? How is our thirst (both physical and spiritual thirst) a good thing in our lives?

— Each day God gives us time, and He wants us to use that time to practice His presence. Think about it. How much time do you spend at the Well each day?

— How much do you love God? How much do you think He loves you? How does our experience of His love enable us to rest?

# Drenched in Prayer

*Father of all comfort, I come to Your Well and trust in Your promise that my burdens will be lifted. You have proven Your love to me in more ways than I can count. Has anyone else ever died for a sinner like me? Has anyone ever loved me more than You? Did I even know love before I met You? Thank You for Your unfailing love today that promises rest for my body, my soul, and my spirit. Help me to quiet myself before You and just drink in Your Spirit that gives freedom and life to my weary being. Amen.*

# Get the Ball Rolling

*When a Samaritan woman came
to draw water Jesus said to her,
"Will you give me a drink?"* [ John 4:7 ]

Have you ever had someone you least expected come up and ask you a question? It gets your immediate attention, doesn't it?

Recently, my football player son-with a great sense of humor, Timmy, and I met an elderly, whiskery man at a nearby fast food restaurant. The man had been praying a blessing over his sausage, egg, and cheese biscuit when, like Jesus, he asked us a simple question in order to get the ball rolling. As he got up from his seat and came over to sit with us, he asked, "How old do you think I am?" His quick inquisition eventually led us to an in-depth conversation in which we learned his life history, the date of his birthday, and that it was supposed to snow on the following Saturday! Unfortunately, we forgot to ask his name...(Ever notice the Samaritan Woman was never mentioned by name either?)

Jesus knew His question would take the Samaritan Woman off guard, because Jewish men didn't speak to Samaritans, and especially Samaritan women. The Samaritans were an intermixed race of Jews and Gentiles—half-breeds who were reviled by the Jews. But Jesus wasn't prejudiced. He was trying to make more than one point that day. Race, culture, economic status, and gender were non-issues with Him. Christ wants all of us to be able to put ourselves in the Samaritan Woman's shoes (or sandals, more likely!), and that's why He never called her by name. But rather than putting ourselves in her shoes, we're usually waiting for the other shoe to drop! It's so comforting to see unconditional love in action.

The little old man at the restaurant took us by surprise as he stood up and asked if he could join us for breakfast. His question was much like Jesus asking the woman for a drink...only on this day, everyone at the restaurant seemed to stand up and take notice—for what I interpreted to be the wrong reasons. It's unfortunate that our society has so much fear from violence and terror. Today, when neighborly love occurs, people get downright uptight with fear rather than relaxed with acceptance. Our minds often operate from a negative viewpoint rather than from the mind of Christ. My son and I welcomed the stranger, awkward as it was at the time. Jesus' conversation at the well was a bit awkward too. At times when I read through the entire story, it reminds me of a tennis match, "One up, love, match point!" The love of God knows no limits, no boundaries, no walls, and never fears. It only perseveres. The elderly man joined us for an intriguing breakfast, and the Samaritan Woman joined Jesus for an intriguing drink from the well that day, both initiated from rather simple questions which got the ball rolling.

Right before Timmy and I left to run our errands, the man asked us another question: "Would you like come to my church for Saturday breakfast?" Just like Jesus, he was an evangelist—the similarities were astonishing to me!

The next Saturday, it snowed (what are the odds?) and we joined him for breakfast at his little (and I do mean *little)* country church. We learned not only his name, "Cami", but also that Cami could cook! The homemade sausage gravy and biscuits melted in our mouths, and the eggs and bacon were much better than the restaurant's!

Can you see the similarities of our stories? The Samaritan Woman came to the well for her physical thirst, but she was dying for love. Jesus met her real need and quenched her spiritual thirst with the Living Water of His love. She joined Jesus, and her cup overflowed with something sweeter than anything she had ever experienced.

In the same way, my son and I went to the restaurant to satisfy our physical hunger, and we ended up involved in a God-sized adventure of faith that would awaken and feed our spiritual hunger. The principles we find in the Bible parallel our experiences today, if we will only explore them, accept them, and utilize them in our own lives.

By the way, we worshipped with Cami and his church family, the following Sunday. What really warmed my heart was their sincerity, their simplicity, and of course, the One we all had in common: Our Savior! (Our hearts were also warmed by the smile on Cami's face when we walked in the door.)

I sure hope when I am as old as Cami, I'm still asking questions, and still inviting people to dine with my Savior, and of course, I hope they still come.

We all look forward to the day when we are invited to the banquet feast of Heaven with God, but let's not forget that He gives us morsels big enough to wet any appetite everyday—if we will only accept His offers.

## Drink the Living Water

"If anyone is thirsty, let him come to me and drink. Whoever believes in me, as the Scripture has said, streams of living water will flow from within him." [John 7:27]

"You prepare a table before me, in the presence of my enemies. You anoint my head with oil, my cup overflows." [Psalm 23:5]

"He has taken me to the banquet hall, and his banner over me is love." [Song of Solomon 2:4]

"When Jesus saw him lying there and learned that he had been in this condition for a long time, he asked him, "Do you want to get well?" [John 5:6]

## Deeper Reflections

— Think of several people you've sat next to in the past few days. What questions can you ask to start a conversation rolling with someone God brings across your path?

— Who are some people you know who are really good listeners? What makes them so good at it? What can you learn from them?

— Jesus was prompted to start a conversation because He loved the woman. Think about your own heart of compassion. When was a time in your life when you were most compassionate toward those in need?

— What might help inflame the fires of compassion in you now?

## Drenched in Prayer

*Faithful Father, You are incredible! I love the way You parallel my life to Your Son's life, giving me opportunities to do some of the things Jesus did—if I'll only see the opportunities around me. Thanks for sending people into my life to keep me channeled in the right direction, and help me Lord, to not be fearful in getting the ball rolling with others by asking simple questions that build relationships. I have nothing to lose, for You have already lost Your life for me that I might have life and enjoy it! Also let me bring You honor and glory today by seeing interruptions in life as opportunities to splash Your Living Water! Amen.*

# In-To-Me-See

*(His disciples had gone into the town to buy food.)* [ John 4:8 ]

I always chuckle when I read this verse. Have you ever sent someone on an errand, to just, well, get rid of him or her for the time being—maybe your husband or your teenager? Okay, okay, I admit I've done it! Jesus had several missions to complete that day. Foremost on His mind was being alone with the Samaritan Woman at the Well, because she probably wouldn't have given Him the time of day—much less her undivided attention—with an audience of all things, men! Yes, men would have been a *major* distraction for her, don't you agree? I'm pretty certain that was Jesus' main reason for sending His disciples for food, because later in the story when they offer Him lunch, He wasn't hungry! Jesus knows us so well, better than we know ourselves, and on this particular day, in mid October or so, He was on a mission that required a private meeting between Him and our Well Woman. Intimacy can be spelled *in-to–me-see!* He was definitely seeing into her when He sent His men disciples away, and that was only the beginning!

When you think about being alone with Jesus today, is it hard for you?

And if so, why?

There are several reasons it might be difficult to spend time alone with Jesus. First, of course, is fear, shame, guilt, or condemnation. Second is time—or the lack thereof. Third is spiritual apathy. Some of us have allowed our passion for Christ to burn out due to lack of spiritual discipline. We're just limping along in our Christian faith, only warming the pew every Sunday, and complacency has set in. Fourth is the desire for stimulation and excitement, which we may or may not receive. We live in a world of tangible sensations. If we don't feel it, we assume it doesn't exist. When we don't sense God's presence, we assume He's not there. But faith believes without seeing, and sometimes that means even without feeling. A fifth reason we neglect to spend time with Jesus is unconfessed sin. *When we ask Jesus to be Lord of our lives, we secure our eternal salvation through grace, but the quality of our relationship with Him still depends on our obedience. Sin that is unconfessed drives a wedge between God, and us just like unresolved conflict drives a wedge between human relationships.*

Jesus confronted all of these issues with our Woman at the Well. He conquered her fear, shame, guilt, and condemnation. If He had been ashamed of her and thought she deserved to live in constant guilt or fear for her actions, or if He wanted to remind her of each gory detail of her sordid love affairs, He would never had made a point of going through Samaria in the first place! Condemning us obviously is not His intention, and it never is. Jesus doesn't want to meet us to put us *down*. That's exactly why He went *up* on the cross, and He always speaks the truth in love.

She might have been in a hurry to fill her water jugs and go back to town, but because of His gentleness and His ability to intrigue her, she made time for Him. And He met her at her place and on her time. Jesus always meets us right where we are. He promises to never leave us or abandon us. He is always with us. He never put Himself above others or on a pedestal of any kind, with the exception of taking up His cross.

Spiritual apathy can be another excuse for not wanting to be alone with Jesus. If you don't feed your faith, it will die. We don't really know what our Samaritan Woman's faith consisted of, but we do know she had a desire deep within her heart that needed to be flooded with the abundant source of Living Water!

I love the fact that Jesus not only knew everything about her, but that He cared enough even in His tiredness to send His disciples away so He could be alone with her. He wanted everything to be perfect for their first *real* encounter together. God often lays out the red carpet for those who are ready to listen and accept Him as their own Savior or to meet Him in the Throne Room where the Living Water flows. A fresh encounter with the Most High God takes us up without putting others or ourselves down.

Have you ever wondered why Jesus didn't hire an awesome praise band, a huge choir that knew how to rock, and maybe some nifty women's speaker (perhaps me!) that could have made the Samaritan Woman ooh and ahh with holy goose bumps? I wonder if sometimes we don't miss the boat when we focus on pageantry in worship instead of searching for Jesus. Stimulation is it's own religion today. We need to pay attention to today's lesson that Jesus desires to be alone with us. A church that manipulates our emotions may give us a quick high, but we may miss the unchanging, everlasting, Most High God.

Later in our story, we'll see how Jesus handled unconfessed sin for this woman. That's where the intimacy really developed! I don't want to give it away before we get there, though. First, we need to develop our thirst.

Speaking of intimacy, I have a big black leather chair with a lap desk I pull up beside me each morning. I bring my caramel latte in my special cup, light a candle or the fireplace, and meet Jesus at the Well. Sometimes I pray, other times I do all the talking, and sometimes I just sit and listen. As I read my Bible and write in my journal, God speaks to me about my day, my cares, my trials, my sins, my joys, my family, and my ministry. There is *nothing—absolutely nothing*—I would rather do in life than sit at the Well with my Jesus, sharing intimacies with Him. There are tough times, too, when it seems problems and distractions threaten to keep me from spending time with Him. Cultivating our inner lives of solitude is extremely important, and it may mean we need to send someone, something, or even some thoughts away so we can be alone with Jesus.

Today, Jesus has sent His disciples to buy food so He can be alone with you! Will you meet Him?

## Drink the Living Water

"Therefore, brothers, since we have confidence to enter the Most Holy Place by the blood of Jesus, by a new and living way opened for us through the curtain, that is his body, and since we have a great priest over the house of God, let us draw near to God with a sincere heart in full assurance of faith, having our hearts sprinkled to cleanse us from a guilty conscience and having our bodies washed with pure water." [Hebrews10: 19-22]

"Therefore, there is now no condemnation for those in Christ Jesus, because through Christ Jesus the law of the Spirit of life set me free from the law of sin and death." [Romans 8:1-2]

"God did this so that men would seek Him and perhaps reach out for Him and find Him, though He is not far from each one of us. For in Him we live and move and have our being." [Acts 17:27-28]

## Deeper Reflections

— Think about each of the reasons why we may avoid spending time with Jesus. Are any of these reasons a problem for you? If so, explain how they distract or intimidate you:

- Fear, shame, guilt, or condemnation—


- Time—


- Spiritual apathy—

- The desire for constant stimulation—

- Unconfessed sin—

— Are you able to practice God's presence daily? What are some of the benefits you'd experience if you spent more time soaking up the Living Water of His presence?

— What are some things that can help you deal effectively with distractions?

## Drenched in Prayer

*Lord, I ask that today You help me to concentrate on You by eliminating distractions and totally submitting my heart to You. You are so worthy of my time, and You want me to spend it with You. Thank You for showing me how much You wanted to eliminate the space and lack of intimacy between us. You saw my lostness, and You gave Your life for me on the cross so that I could be having intimacy and abundant life with You today. In the beautiful name of Jesus, I pray. Amen.*

# Putting God in a Box

*You are a Jew and I am a Samaritan, how can you ask me for a drink? (For Jews do not associate with Samaritans.)* [ John 4:9 ]

et me paraphrase the woman's question. She was asking, "You're God, and I'm a mere human being. How can you ask me for anything? I mean, really, God?"

Do you ever do this? Do you praise God for who He is, and then question His right to intervene in *your* life? Or after God gives you direction to do something, do you tell Him how incapable you are—not to mention worthless and just plain pitiful? Do you ever ask God how He can possibly ask one more thing of you, much less put one more trial, hardship or suffering in your path?

Recently I was talking with of all things the "waterman" (we were getting a water softener installed). As he recited his present hardships to me, he mentioned that he thought, "God was never supposed to give you more than you could handle." This is a prime example of the many ways we try to put God in a box. Just like the Samaritan Woman, we say, "I'm telling you today, God, that you're God, and You're not supposed to give me any more than I can handle because You said that You love me. And I'm quite sure *I know best* just how much I can handle, so why are you allowing all this to happen?" This question is much like the Woman at the Well's question to Jesus: "You are a Jew and I am a Samaritan, how can you ask me for a drink?"

The waterman realized that sometimes our perspective needs to be realigned. Before we go any further, I must tell you that the Bible promises us that God won't let us be tempted beyond what we can bear. In 1 Corinthians 10:13, Paul assures us, "No temptation has seized you except what is common to man. And God is faithful; He will not let you be tempted beyond what you can bear. But when you are tempted, He will also provide a way out so that you can stand up under it." But in my experience and the experience of countless believers over the centuries, sometimes God gives us more than we *think* we can handle for exactly that reason: He wants us to understand that He is in control; not us. (Ahaa, what a novel idea!) *God gives us a need or two or three that we can't handle, and then gives us Himself!* God's objective isn't our comfort. His divine purpose is to increase our faith. He accomplishes that goal by stretching us beyond what we think we can bear so we'll learn to trust Him more.

Also, God has other objectives for bringing difficulties into our lives. Building our trust is a reward for our willingness to be obedient. Also, He uses our trials to showcase His glory, His miracles, and His love. Life comes from death, and difficulties cause us to die a little bit to ourselves, that is, to trust less in our own wisdom and strength and trust more in God's character and power. Since Christ is our example, why wouldn't we be asked to suffer once in a while? Isn't that what makes us take up our cross and follow Him?

Christian apologist and author C. S. Lewis said, "God cannot use a man (or woman) greatly, until He has wounded him deeply." When I experience severe trials, I sometimes wonder what's wrong with me. I think to myself, "Maybe I'm not trying hard enough or trying too hard, or maybe I'm not good enough," or I wonder, "Perhaps I've done something wrong, and I don't even know it. Maybe I'm being attacked by enemy, or maybe both." Can you relate to these kinds of mental and spiritual gymnastics? But if I think about it long enough, I know better. I have faith that God knows right where I am, and He will provide the grace to get me through. Do you believe that today in your present circumstances? It makes all the difference in the world!

The waterman told me about a process called "reverse osmosis." I thought to myself, "That's it! Reverse the bad, and keep the good!" It's so important to run our thoughts through the Well of Living Water—without telling God who *we think* He is and what *we think* we need. Instead, we can focus on *knowing* Who He is, focusing our minds on the truth of His Word, and asking Him for what we *know* is His will. Things don't always appear as they really are. We live in a tangible world, but the unseen, intangible world is just as real. We need spiritual eyes to see the unseen. Let's be good stewards of the Word of God by asking Him to show us the Truth and to expose the lies in our minds and hearts.

Don't put God in a box today. Valleys are just as much a part of God's plan as the mountaintops.

- Without the valleys, we wouldn't appreciate the mountaintops.
- Without the valleys, we may not relate to other people who are having a difficult time.

- Without the valleys, we would have no empathy for what others are feeling.
- Without the valleys, we may not learn what the Lord wishes to teach us.
- Without the valleys, we can't pass on what we learn to others.
- Without the valleys, we may see ourselves as perfect or above others.
- Without the valleys, we can't work through some of our emotions and feelings.
- Without the valleys, some of these motivationals wouldn't exist.
- Without the valley of death, God's glory would never have been showcased through Jesus, who died so we could live!

## Drink the Living Water

"Even though I walk through the valley of the shadow of death, I will fear no evil." [Psalm 23:4]

"We must go through many hardships to enter the kingdom of God." [Acts 14:22]

"See to it that no one takes you captive through hollow and deceptive philosophy, which depends on human tradition and the basic principles of this world rather than on Christ." [Colossians 2:8]

## *Deeper Reflections*

— How do people around you usually respond to difficulties in their lives? How do you normally respond?


— What difference would it make to genuinely believe that the difficulties are part of God's divine plan to strengthen our faith and draw us closer to Himself?


— Our view of God often comes from our earthly father, which may be incorrect. What characteristics does your Heavenly Father have that your earthly father does not?


— Are you prone to do all the talking when you're praying to God? Do you often tell Him how you want your prayers answered and when, or are you a good listener when you pray?


— What valleys or mountaintops have you experienced lately? Did you wait on the Lord for wisdom, or were you quick to tell Him what you thought He should be doing?

## *Drenched in Prayer*

*Dear Father, valleys are part of life and part of Your plan to refine me as gold, test me, try me, and ultimately form me into Your Son's image. It's going to be okay. Since my valleys bring me closer to You, Lord, help me to see them as good and valuable. You are the Almighty Creator, the God of the mountaintops as well as Lord of the valleys. You have me engraved on the palm of Your hand, and I'm covered by Your wings of faithfulness. Help me to see You not as I've thought You were, but as You really are. Amen.*

## *Dipping Out to Others*

If you are fortunate enough to be on the mountaintop today, rest in His love, and pray for those in the valleys! And if you're in the valley, pray for yourself and those around you, too! We are happy to take your prayer request at our website today: www.womenofthewell.org

# *Personalized Prayer*

*Jesus answered her, "If you knew the gift of God and who it is that asks you for a drink, you would have asked Him and He would have given you living water."* [ John 4:10 ]

his may be my favorite verse of all time. I love the way the Master Storyteller weaves a story. In the verse before this, the Samaritan Woman asked Jesus the question: "How can You ask me for a drink?" The woman was talking about physical $H_2O$ that came from Jacob's well. Jesus changed the course of the conversation by his statement, including *"if, what, who, how, and ask."* Of course, He was referring to something totally foreign to her, called "Living Water," spiritual water for her soul. The metaphorical significance is important to our story.

Isn't it just like Jesus to totally captivate His audience? We should take notes from this Man who called fishermen to become followers, and they immediately dropped their nets when He said, "Come follow me." No problem, no questions asked! Now, here at verse ten in our drama, Jesus throws out another one-liner to His audience at the well in order to bring her life, freedom, and peace. The irony of this moment is that the woman thought Jesus wanted something from her. Not! He wanted to give her the most precious thing in life—a personal, one-on-one relationship.

Isn't it just like Jesus to answer the woman's question with a gift? When we go to the Well to meet Jesus, He's already waiting to give us the gifts He has stored up for us in heaven. Sometimes He doesn't answer just the way we want, but yes, He answers. Recently, someone sent me a clipping called "This I know..." (I apologize, the author wasn't listed.)

> *I know not by what methods are, but this I know, God answers prayer.*
> *I know that He has given His Word, which tells me prayer is always heard*
> *and will be answered soon or late, and so I pray and calmly wait.*
> *I know not if the blessing sought will come in just the way I thought,*
> *but leave my prayers with Him alone, whose will is wiser than my own,*
> *assured that He will grant my quest and send some answer far more blest.*

I'm convinced that most of us aren't aware of God's gifts just waiting for us. But *if* we knew *what* they were, and *Who* they were coming from, we would *ask* more often, for that explains how we receive them! To know Him is to know His gifts and how extravagantly He loves us.

God is saying to you and me, "If you knew all the gifts of your inheritance in Christ Jesus, you would be spending a lot more time in prayer asking for them." If we aren't aware the gifts are available, we probably won't ask for them. In this passage, Jesus is saying, "Even though you don't know, or even understand, ask anyway!" He has given us the deepest desires of our hearts, and He longs to fulfill those desires.

When was the last time you asked Him a question and ended up with a gift? Jesus Christ is the ultimate gift giver of all time. He gave His life to save us from our sins. He gave His Holy Spirit to counsel us. He gave His stories to help us understand His truth. He gave thousands of people fish and bread for dinner. He gave the disciples a legacy to pass on to others. He gave Mary and Martha their brother back. He gave the blind man sight. He gave and He gave and He gave. Actually, He gave Himself right into the grave. As we seek Him, the gifts of peace, love, and joy naturally flow from Him to us like water in a stream.

On that day in Jesus' conversation with the Woman at the Well, He was about to give her the gift of Living Water. But I believe what this particular verse offers us is the gift of *personalized prayer*. He was saying, "Ask for what you think you need, and I'll give you what I know is best." Don't be afraid to ask for anything you desire, but don't put Him in a box either! We pray, and He personalizes it to fit us perfectly. We can't meet with Him in human form as the Samaritan Woman did, but we have the examples of His encounter in the Bible, and we have the Holy Spirit to speak to our hearts. He's just waiting for us to ask.

# Drink the Living Water

"In the same way the Spirit helps us in our weakness. We do not know what we ought to pray for, but the Spirit himself intercedes for us with groans that words cannot express. And he who searches our hearts knows the mind of the Sprit, because the Spirit intercedes for the saints in accordance with God's will." [Romans 8:26-27]

"You want something but don't get it. You kill and covet, but you cannot have what you want. You quarrel and fight. You do not have, because you do not ask God. When you ask, you do not receive because you ask with wrong motives, that you may spend what you get on your pleasures." [James 4:2-3]

"During the days of Jesus' life on earth, He offered up prayers and petitions with loud cries and tears to the one who could save Him from death, and He was heard because of His reverent submission." [Hebrews 5:7]

# Deeper Reflections

— What do you need today: peace, comfort, love, a friend, an answer to a pressing question, counsel, or joy? God is listening…go ahead and ask Him. Then wait in silence and listen for His answer.

— What does your prayer time consist of? Is it truly personal, and if not, why not?

— Are you drinking deeply of Living Water? Have you ever asked God for the Living Water? (See appendix A in the back of the book, for notes on how to ask Jesus into your heart if you have a need for salvation.)

## Drenched in Prayer

*Merciful Father, I repent of unfaithfulness in my prayer life. What a gift You have given me! And yet it's a gift I often neglect or forget. Forgive me today, and fill me instead with the Living Water of Your love. Amen.*

## Dipping Out to Others
Pray today for a friend.

# The Water and the Invitation

# Go Deep!

*"Sir," the woman said, "you have nothing to draw with and the well is deep."* [ John 4:11 ]

*eep water.* What do you think about when someone says "deep water"? Fishing? Swimming? Snorkeling? Jaws? When Jesus speaks of deep water, He thinks of something far beyond our comprehension, for His ways are higher...and deeper... than anything we can imagine. In our society, we think we have to know absolutely everything, but the will and the ways of an infinite God are beyond our finite minds. Let's not limit God to only what we can understand.

Twenty some years ago, I lived in Islamorada, the sport fishing capital of the world, located in the Florida Keys. My girlfriend Liz and I often went out on a "party boat" on the weekends to fish. We had a lot of fun, and I enjoyed her company tremendously. Liz was a spitfire—always ready for anything! The captain often took a boat-load of us to "The Point," miles out on the deep blue ocean where no land could be seen. We fished for a species of fish called yellow tail. Catching yellow tail takes a special "touch," which I'm proud to say my friend and I both had! Quite honestly, we made the men on the boat a little jealous! We let our fishing lines out just right, not too fast, not too slow, anticipating any slight tug that might be a fish biting the bait. Then, when we felt a bump or a bite, we had to decide whether to yank the line, wait and let out more line, or just reel it on in. Oh, we had a blast! And those fish are delicious to eat! Yum, I can taste them now! Deep-sea fishing is fun and adventurous. I even had my own home-made yellow tailing rod with my name on it. (In case you're interested, my largest catch was a 185 pound tuna, caught in the deep beautiful blue waters of Hawaii, and that's no fisherman's tall tale! Who said women can't fish? I've made my dad proud!)

The great news is that God's kingdom is just as exciting! His Well of love is so deep. If we will only let our fishing lines out, we can reel in as much as our spirits can take. In our story about the Woman at the Well, Jesus was drawing a vivid picture that He had nothing to draw water with. We, too, sometimes feel we have nothing to draw spiritual life with, don't we? We just don't have it in us. We feel empty, helpless, and hopeless. Perhaps we really don't know how to submit ourselves to God, acknowledge our brokenness, and allow God to fill us. Many times, we look to others first in order to fill our spiritual Wells. Or we play games of complaining, blaming, comparing, jealousy or envy. We always come up empty when we resort to these methods. The only sure source is to draw from Jesus through His Word and receive spiritual nourishment through the Bible, prayer, church, or Bible studies. Can you imagine what the world would be like if everyone got up in the morning and spent time at the Well until they were filled to overflowing with the love of Jesus? Traffic jams would be different, waiting in lines would be different, our thought processes would change, and our compassion and understanding would skyrocket! Mercy would lead the way!

We long to have our spiritual thirst quenched, and that kind of drink is found in the Word of God, page after page, ripple after ripple of thirst-quenching goodness. The source is Jesus Christ Himself, and His fountain of *Gushing Springs* never runs dry. Where else can you go and receive mercy for your shortcomings and walk away refreshed and renewed, or find company just when you feel alone or desperate?

It's interesting that Jesus originally called men who were fishermen to follow Him, but at the empty tomb, He gave the women the Good News of His resurrection power! Could it be that He saw the men were able to wait patiently because that was a requirement in their fishing careers? In patiently listening to their Lord and His instructions, they fished in deep spiritual waters. Just as deep-sea fishing takes a fishing pole and a constant determination to catch fish, so it is in the spiritual dimension. It takes a Bible, perseverance, and patience to glean those spiritual truths from the depths of God's Word. Seek and you shall catch, and then you, too, can go and share the Good News!

Sometimes we read the Word nonchalantly, without even thinking about the meaning of the passage we're reading. If we pay attention, however, we may detect the Someone who can quench our thirst each day. The joy of fishing depends on the deep waters you are fishing in and the Captain of your boat!

I remember one day when I went "fishing" in God's Word. It was one of those "crazy mother" days when I had had about enough. Everything had gone wrong! I actually thought that if I heard another discontented child say "Mommy" one more time, I'd lose my mind! I opened God's Word to Acts 26:25, and it calmed my thoughts. I concluded, "I'm not insane!" No kidding! God can speak to us when we least expect it!

After the loss of my sister, I received an email from a woman who had read one of my lessons. She included a verse that spoke to my heart, and I knew it was sent directly by God. (2 Corinthians 7:8) My sister and I had exchanged letters before her death. Though the woman who sent me the note had no idea my sister and I had passed letters, her note mentioned the importance of letters shared by people and how as Christians we can live with no regrets. Her note meant so much to me! I can't tell you how incredibly deep God's Word goes, but I will tell you He cares, He loves you, and He knows exactly what's going on in your life. I could tell stories of how His Word has soothed me, calmed me, instructed me and loved me for hours, but that's another book!

I encourage you to go deep today by asking God questions such as *where, who, why,* and *what?* You won't regret the time you've spent exploring the heights of His love and the depths of His Well!

# *Drink the Living Water*

"The words of a man's mouth are deep waters, but the fountain of wisdom is a bubbling brook." [Proverbs 18:4]

"For the Word of God is living and active. Sharper than any double-edged sword, it penetrates even to dividing souls and spirit, joints and marrow; it judges the thoughts and attitudes of the heart." [Hebrews 4:12]

"In the beginning was the Word, and the Word was with God, and the Word was God." [John 1:1]

"The days are coming, " declares the Sovereign Lord, "when I will send a famine through the land--not a famine of food or a thirst for water, but a famine of hearing the words of the Lord." [Amos 8:11-14]

## *Deeper Reflections*

— Have you ever compared the depths of the ocean to the vastness and depth of God's Word? Ponder it for a few moments. What similarities do you find?

— Describe the richest insight from God's Word you have enjoyed in the past week or so. How did that insight affect your attitude and actions?

— Do you have trouble paying close attention when you read the Bible? If you do, what can you do to stay mentally sharp as you read?

— Take a few minutes now to thank God for the richness of His Word.

## Drenched in Prayer

*Lord, Your Word is so deep. Thank You for Your gift that keeps on giving! It's such a freedom to be able to pick up Your Word each day and fish through its pages in expectation of what You have for me. I stand amazed at how many times I can read a passage and still learn from it. Motivate me to memorize passages that will help me in time of need, and to share Your Words with others daily. It's my desire to go deep! Amen.*

*Where?*

*"Where can you get this living water?"*

[ John 4:11 ]

And the question is the same for us: Where can *we* get this Living Water? Aren't we glad our Samaritan Woman had the guts to ask? Do you ever ask God tough questions? It's okay. He can take it, believe me!

The deep Well of Living Water, however, might not be found where you think it is. You might imagine it in the middle of the Sahara Desert, or in a dusty, barren land filled with prickly cactus, or perhaps a vibrant, crystal clear fountain of youth somewhere in romantic Paris or Rome. Some may even picture it as a special holy water that has been blessed inside the church.

The beautiful picture painted in John's gospel is meant to be a stained glass window of "our state of inner being" as we approach the Well of Living Water. It's a picture of brokenness, unquenchable thirst, true desire for more, and a neediness that we can't explain. One of the ways our thirst is expressed is in desperate statements and questions, such as: "Why does all this stuff happen to me?" "What did I do wrong?" "Where can I find relief?" "Isn't there more to life?" "Why me?" "What if…?" "If only…" And the list goes on and on.

God has taken me to many different Scripture passages to answer the question of where we can find Living Water. When that question is answered, many of the other questions fall into place like a pristine waterfall. I visited the Well for hours this morning and was really thrilled when God led me to my own "gushing spring" in the book of Habakkuk, a book that explains that many of our problems are the result of our limited understanding about God. The theme of Habakkuk is laid out through the same format as the Woman at the Well: question and answers. We find that our knowledge of truth is always tested. In summary, we have problems, God has the plan, we complain and protest, but God has a different perspective. The golden strand that pulls it altogether is prayer! (Or simply asking God, and waiting for His answers.)

Habakkuk 2:1 tells us, "I will stand at my watch and station myself on the ramparts; I will look to see what He will say to me, and what answer I am to give to this complaint." Several prophets of the Old Testament used the watchtower and the watchman to illustrate an attitude of expectancy. We find the Living Water when we have an attitude of expectancy. Habakkuk patiently waited for God's response and watched for Him, too. We tend to want everything *now* in our instant culture, though, don't we? I love Habakkuk because he positioned himself intentionally to best receive God's message, which were answers to his complaints. The watchtower was high above the city, and it allowed him to see the enemies that could hinder his progress.

I then looked at Habakkuk 3:19, which says, "The Sovereign Lord is my strength; He makes my feet like the feet of a deer, He enables me to go on the heights." But sometimes we don't like to go on the heights, do we? Ever heard the song, "As the Deer Pants for Water"? The poor deer (no pun intended!) is panting because it's going up the rocky, hard places, climbing the tallest mountain to the heights of glory. We, too, pant for the Living Water as we seek God in His glory. This verse is important because we must learn to embrace our thirsts for Jesus and not run from our trials. Where is the Well? It's the presence of God where He shares His love and comfort in the daily stuff of life. We also find the Well in times of suffering as we position ourselves with expectancy through reflection and solitude.

Next, God took me into the New Testament. 1 Corinthians 6:19 reminds us that our bodies are temples of the Holy Spirit. Ephesians 2:6 tells us: "And God raised us up with Christ and seated us with Him in the heavenly realms in Christ Jesus, in order that in the coming ages He might show the incomparable riches of his grace, expressed in His kindness to us in Christ Jesus." Here, the Well of Living Water is found within us, as well as high and lifted up with Him! This is a parallel of the Habakkuk verses.

God is telling us, *"When you see yourself seated in the heavenly places, your body washed clean by the blood of Jesus, believing and expecting the Spirit to move within you, willing to wait with expectancy, you will find the Well of Living Water. There you will find more than answers to your questions."* Jesus waits for us to approach the throne of grace where Gushing Springs flow as we bow humbly and expectantly. We can come boldly, but only because we now possess righteousness that was credited to our account by Jesus. Seek and you shall find the Well, within, high up, in Christ, through love!

## *Drink the Living Water*

"As the deer pants for streams of water, so my soul pants for you, O God. My soul thirsts for God, for the living God. When can I go and meet with God?" [Psalm 42:1-2]

"For with you is the fountain of life; in your light we see light." [Psalm 36:9]

"I wait for the Lord, my soul waits, and in His Word I put my hope. My soul waits for the Lord more than watchmen wait for the morning, more than watchmen wait for the morning. O Israel, put your hope in the Lord, for with the Lord is unfailing love and with Him is full redemption." [Psalm 130:5-7]

## *Deeper Reflections*

— Like Habakkuk in the watchtower, are you able to see your enemies as they are approaching? How can you spot troublesome times in your life?

— Are you like the deer, panting for more of the Living Water as it climbs the mountains of life? Or are you more like a kitty cat—just wanting to drink from the bowl in the kitchen on the flat floor? Explain your answer.

— Have you truly embraced your thirst for the Living Water? Often we don't drink if we aren't thirsty, and sometimes we are drinking other things that eventually won't satisfy. What things do you need to get out of the way in order to jump-start your thirst?

— What questions do you have for God? And can you find the Living Water?

## Drenched in Prayer

*Lord, sometimes I just don't know where to find You, and yet You have promised to never leave me or forsake me! Help me to always remember You are only a breath away and that I live and breathe in You. When I have so many questions and complaints, may I trust You, because You are always more than enough. Forgive my unwillingness to wait upon You with expectancy, and grant me patience. Amen.*

# Who?

*"Are you greater than our father Jacob, who gave us the well and drank from it himself, as did also his sons and his flocks and herds?"*

[ John 4:12 ]

We need to put this question in perspective. Our Woman at the Well blurted out this question after she had asked Jesus, "Where can you get this Living Water?" Some people see her as an ignorant peasant, but I believe she was a lot smarter than most people think. Good questions serve as spiritual stethoscopes. Her question first asked "where?" and now "who?" She was a bit gutsy. In effect, she was asking Jesus, "Just who do you think you are?" To some of us, her question seems arrogant, but I believe she was asking because her heart was parched and dry. She was desperate to connect with someone who could give her some answers. As we know, she had experienced a lot of rejection and loneliness. Many people with her background are bitter, unforgiving, and resentful, with symptoms of anger and despair. They question the truth and often believe lies, thinking they are truth. Her third question to Jesus was probably the most important one. She is finally asking what she desperately needs to know: "Okay, let's get down to business, just tell me who you *r-e-a-l-l-y* are."

Her earnestness showed her true heart. She knew in her heart of hearts that she was missing something, and she wanted to make sure she didn't miss her chance again. Many people put this woman down for her divorces and affairs, but her mind was sharp enough to figure out that this was a once-in-a-lifetime trip to the Well. She wasn't going to miss it.

"Are you greater?" she asked. In other words, "Can you be trusted?" "Will You let me down like those five husbands I've had?" She was also asking, "And by the way, what do You want from me? What can you offer me that the other men couldn't fulfill?" We are just like her. We want to figure it all out, get the answers up front, decide if A + B is going to = C, or look for a program that has a guarantee of smooth sailing forever. I imagine her mind was reeling with questions. She wanted some answers at the beginning of their conversation. Many of us have been in her shoes, but the story doesn't end here, does it? Even though she was seeking answers, it was her question that opened the door to Living Water.

It's not about asking the right questions or getting the right answers. It's about Jesus. Her first two words were: "Are You...?" She wanted to know about Jesus. She wasn't seeking the answers as much as she was seeking Him. He knew her heart was crusty and thirsty for Him.

I once told someone about Jesus, and she said to me, "I don't understand it all." My answer to her, which I know was from God, was, "I don't understand it all, either, but I do know one thing: that we must believe first and then understanding will follow."

God is greater—greater than all the sands of the beach, greater than all the stars in the sky, and greater than any number you can fathom. He can't be unfaithful, because He is faithfulness. Rely on Him today, for He is greater than anyone, anything, any circumstance, and any reason to doubt Him. Seek Him. In fact, seek Him more than you seek the answers to your questions, because He is the Living Water. Let's take a look at who God says He is by looking at His own Words in the book of John:

- He is the Son of Man (John 6:27),
- He is the Bread of Life (6:35),
- He is the Light of the World (8:12),
- He is the Gate for the sheep (10:7),
- He is the Good Shepherd (10:11),
- He is the resurrection and the life (11:25),
- He is the way and the truth and the life (14:6), and
- He is the vine (15:1).

And now let's look at His key characteristics which are scattered throughout the entire the first four gospels, (Matthew, Mark, Luke and John):

- Jesus is the Son of God; Jesus is God who became human, the Christ, and the Messiah.
- Jesus came to help sinners and has power to forgive sins. He has authority over death.

- Jesus has power to give eternal life and heal the sick. Jesus taught with authority and was compassionate. Jesus experienced sorrow and never, ever disobeyed God.

Lastly let's take a look at what Jesus is called in the last book of the Bible, the Book of Revelation:
- The Alpha and the Omega (1:8)
- Lord God (1:8)
- The Almighty (1:8)
- Son of Man (1:13)
- The First and the Last (1:17)
- The Living One (1:18)
- Son of God (2:18)
- Witness (3:14)
- Creator (4:11)
- Lion of the tribe of Judah (5:5)
- Root of David (5:5)
- Lamb (5:6)
- Shepherd (7:17)
- Christ (12:10)
- Faithful and True (19:11)
- Word of God (19:13)
- King of kings (19:16)
- Lord of lords (19:16)
- The Morning Star (22:16)

At one point, Jesus asked His disciples a simple but profound question. I think He's asking the same question to you and me today: "Who do you say I am?"

## Drink the Living Water

"Those who turn away from you will be written in the dust because they have forsaken the Lord, the spring of living water." [Jeremiah 17:13]

"The name of the Lord is a strong tower; the righteous run into it and are safe." [Proverbs 18:10]

"I consider everything a loss compared to the surpassing greatness of knowing Christ Jesus my Lord, for whose sake I have lost all things." [Philippians 3:8]

## Deeper Reflections

— As you think about the woman's background, what are some reasons she may have been defensive when Jesus began a conversation with her?

— What are some misconceptions many people have about Jesus? How might their backgrounds shape those misconceptions?

— When might arrogance be an attempt to cover up insecurity?

— Think about the descriptive phrases and words about Jesus in this lesson, and answer the questions: Who do you say Jesus is? Do you feel you know Him in an intimate way?

— Do you trust Him or do you still have fleeting doubts and questions? Explain your answer.

— How do the descriptions and names for Christ in this lesson address your questions and doubts?

## Drenched in Prayer

*Oh Everlasting Father, I want to know You more and more each day! Open my eyes to who You really are, and help me never to quit searching for the depths of Your love. You are love, and I want to dwell in Your love today. Thank You for Your awesomeness and Your might, Your sovereignty and Your faithfulness to me. Amen.*

# Why?

*Jesus answered, "Everyone who drinks this water will be thirsty again..."* [ John 4:13 ]

Some of us are spiritually thirsty all day every day. If that's the case, perhaps we're drinking from the wrong well. Jeremiah 2:13 says, "My people have committed two sins: They have forsaken me, the spring of living water, and have dug their own cisterns, broken cisterns that cannot hold water."

Many of us have turned to broken cisterns that simply can't hold water. They look like they could be Wells of Living Water, but they are empty, and they leave us thirsty. Broken cisterns in our lives might be status, education, children, power, material things, financial wealth, titles, recognition, busyness, fame, drugs, alcohol, food, sex, pornography...just to name a few. Obviously, not all of these are harmful or sinful in themselves, (although some are), but each of them can be destructive if we put them at the center of our desires and try to use them to quench our thirst. They weren't designed for that purpose.

I spent some time thinking and praying about this issue of broken cisterns, and the insight God gave me was surprising. The Bible says our hearts are deceitful above all things, and one of the ways it has deceived many of us is to think we can receive *fresh water* from going to church, reading books, listening to sermons, attending conferences, watching DVDs or television evangelism, and seminars about God. Don't get me wrong! I'm in ministry. You're reading this either on the Internet or in a book, and hopefully it's leading you to God. But it's intended to do just that: lead you to God, but not take the place of God in your life! These things (sermons, conferences, retreats, DVDs, books and seminars) certainly aren't wrong or evil. In fact, they can be useful tools in God's hands to shape people's lives. But they should never take the place of God in our hearts. It's God who does the shaping, it's God who causes growth, and it's God who deserves the credit for changed lives. When we're seeking to make God our *priority,* looking for Jesus' *perspective,* and walking in the Holy Spirit's *power,* transformation will take place. We need to commune with God for ourselves regularly. I call these "communions" my daily trips to the Well.

When we're trying to get water from broken cisterns, something is always missing. Jesus came to "bind up the brokenhearted." We live in a fallen world, and we'll always have a crack or two! It's our motive, our humility, that He is looking at. Are we seeking Him, and are we growing in Him?

Think of it as buying stocks from a stockbroker. Something is missing when you cash in, even if it grew during the duration of deposit. A broker always takes a commission from the principle. It's the same thing with our devotional times. If we always rely on a preacher, reading a book, or tuning in to a radio personality, we may receive some water, but it will never be the same as the real, fresh, Living Water that Jesus intends for us to enjoy. We will still come away a bit thirsty. Getting God's Word for yourself, well… there's no substitute. I don't know about you, but I want the real thing.

Now humor me for a moment! The television commercial I picture includes two women. One is a woman drinking from a bottle of water that comes from a huge, concrete, water treatment plant. The other woman drinks a bottle from an artesian spring that is gushing from the ground: blue, clear, bubbling, and surrounded by lush green jungle plants and fragrant flowers! One woman paid for her bottle. It quenches some of her thirst, but it leaves her wanting more. The other woman sought out the real spring, and it tasted totally and truly refreshing. She wondered why it took her so long to find it for herself in the first place. There was no comparison. The first was good and did the job on the surface, but the second was incredible, real, inviting, and free for her taking, satisfying her real inner need, and quenching her thirst. Get the picture? The true difference is that Jesus paid the price for the second. It was free, and it was the real thing.

Discipline is an essential ingredient to develop the fruit of the Spirit of self-control. Our thirst often leads us to seek, our seeking urges us to be disciplined, and the outcome leads to *Gushing Springs* of Living Water! In 2 Timothy 1:7, Paul wrote, "For God did not give us a spirit of timidity, but a spirit of power, of love and of self-discipline."

I believe one of our main deterrents to spiritual apathy or getting off the path is to cultivate a disciplined life with Christ. Let me give you my kindergarten formula for discipline. It works for me, and it just may work for you!

C-oncentrate on Jesus

D-elegate to others

E-liminate the unnecessary

Pretty simple, huh? Why not try it for yourself?

# *Drink the Living Water*

"Do you not know that your body is a temple of the Holy Spirit, who is in you, whom you have received from God? You are not your own; you were bought at a price." [1 Corinthians 6:19-20]

"Therefore this is what the Lord says: 'If you repent, I will restore you that you may serve me; if you utter worthy, not worthless, words, you will be my spokesman.'" [Jeremiah 15:19]

"But we have this treasure in jars of clay to show that this all-surpassing power is from God and not from us." [2 Corinthians 4:7]

"The desert and the parched land will be glad; the wilderness will rejoice and blossom. Like the crocus it will burst into bloom; it will rejoice greatly and shout for joy. Water will gush forth in the wilderness and streams in the desert. The burning sand will become a pool, the thirsty ground bubbling springs." [Isaiah 35:1,6-7]

## *Deeper Reflections*

— What are some "broken cisterns" that promise to make us happy and fulfilled but are genuinely destructive?

— What are some "broken cisterns" that are very helpful if we see them as gifts from God, but are harmful if we put them in the center of our lives?

— What "things" do you seek other than God? What are your leaks?

— Would you think of depriving yourself of food when you are hungry? If not, then why would you deprive yourself of spiritual water when you are spiritually thirsty?

— Are you seeking God for yourself, or are you relying only on spiritual content from television, radio, and books?

— What can you delegate or eliminate in your life, in order to help you concentrate on Jesus?

## *Drenched in Prayer*

*Holy Father, forgive me for all the ways I have tried and tried and still try to fill my life with poor substitutes, idols, and things that mean nothing. Cleanse me with Your Living Water, Your blood shed for my sins, and bring me a fresh, new revelation of what it means to seek Your face. Bring me a fresh encounter with the Living God today. Amen.*

# *But What?*

*"…but whoever drinks the water I give will never be thirsty. The water I give will become a spring of water gushing up inside that person, giving eternal life."* [ John 4:14 (NCV) ]

The "but" in Jesus' statement has huge implications for us! Jesus, as the fountain of Living Water, provides the grace that cleanses our sins, provides the insight to make wise decisions, and transforms us through the power of the Holy Spirit within us—*therefore,* quenching our inner thirsts. Have you stopped to *"but drink"* today? Take a few minutes to reflect on these statements about the transforming power of Living Water.

Got Living Water?
Living Water is persistent,
though my faith is not finished.

Living Water is plentiful,
though the world is without hope.
Living Water is profound,
though my conversations may be shallow.
Living Water is passionate,
though I lean toward perfectionism.
Living Water is peaceful,
though at times I am fearful and anxious.
Living Water is patient,
though the love I witness is conditional.
Living Water is powerful,
though I tend to be pitiful.
Living Water is pardoning,
though I deserve the ultimate punishment.
Living Water is perfect,
though I am a work in progress.
Living Water is personal,
though many rituals and ceremonies are not.
Living Water is penetrating,
though my soul is yearning.

So how do we drink this Living Water? How do we dip into this spring-fed Well? I prefer not to give a set agenda, a program, or a list of rules—because these are precisely what Jesus didn't do with the Woman at the Well. We drink through faith! Consider this acrostic that helps draw us to Jesus:

W-alk toward Him.

A-ccept His invitation.

T-rust in His forgiveness.

E-xclaim your love for Him.

R-efresh yourself daily in His care.

Jesus promised eternal life, but what is that? Eternal life begins the moment we accept Christ and start living in the spiritual realm as well as the natural realm. At that moment, we receive the Holy Spirit, and He seals us for eternity. Water is one of the symbols of the Spirit. Christ didn't ignore the natural realm; He was simply using a physical need as a springboard to highlight a spiritual truth. She knew she would be thirsty again, just like He knew that His love lasts forever. He knew the world she lived in would always let her down, while He would never abandon her. He used the common, everyday elements of life with the Samaritan Woman to restore and awaken her thirst to the spiritual life. Eternal life is meant to be abundant; it redeems the old and makes things new. Christ died, that we could live! It is a forever relationship with God. We possess it by believing and following after our Lord Jesus Christ, and when we do, we too will gush springs of Living Water to others!

Women of the Well Ministry exists in order to awaken spiritual sensitivity, help women to embrace their thirst, and find the Gushing Springs of Living Water in Jesus Christ. This transformation happens when the well of emptiness is replaced with the Well of truth and grace of Christ. This Well then lives within us and can be accessed at any time of any day. We never have to drink from other wells that do not satisfy. It is my sincere hope that if you have never accepted Jesus' invitation to drink the Living Water, you will accept Him into your heart today. Trust and follow Him. Live satisfied! *Refuse to trade in what your heart can know and love for what your eyes can see.*

# Drink the Living Water

"Come, all you who are thirsty, come to the waters; and you who have no money, come, buy and eat! Come, buy wine and milk without money and without cost. Why spend your money on what is not bread, and your labor on what does not satisfy? Listen, listen to me, and eat what is good, and your soul will delight in the richest of fare. Give ear and come to me; hear me, that your soul may live. I will make an everlasting covenant with you, my faithful love promised to David." [Isaiah 55:1-3]

"For my Father's will is that everyone who looks to the Son and believes in Him shall have eternal life, and I will raise him up at the last day." [John 6:40]

"For the wages of sin is death, but the gift of God is eternal life in Christ Jesus our Lord." [Romans 6:23]

"Keep yourselves in God's love as you wait for the mercy of our Lord Jesus Christ to bring you to eternal life." [Jude 1:21]

# Deeper Reflections

— Before you read this lesson, how would you have described eternal life? How would you describe it now? Is it attractive to you? Why or why not?

— Is Jesus a spring of water welling up inside of you that causes you to overflow daily into the lives of others?

— Have you often thought you only needed to drink one time, and then you were done? If so, how has that affected your spiritual life and your expectations of God?

— We are all broken vessels, and we need to constantly drink of the Well of Living Water. What are the implications of that fact in your life?

## Drenched in Prayer

*Father, I believe Your Son Jesus died for me. I'm a sinner in need of cleansing. Please wash away my sins, past, present and future as I receive Your gift of eternal life into my heart. Fill me to overflowing with Your mercy and Your love, and help me to follow You and make You the Lord of my life daily. I look forward to becoming a new creation in Christ, and spending eternity with You. Amen.*

# The Honesty and the Acceptance

# Bring It On!

*"Sir, give me this water so that I won't get thirsty and have to keep coming here to draw water."* [ John 4:15 ]

After the woman has all her questions answered, she spurts out exactly what Jesus wanted to hear: "Bring on the water!" She politely asked for His gift by calling Him, "Sir," but oh, there was a catch. Before we find out what the trouble was, let me share a glimpse of my life.

Almost every morning, I have the rare pleasure of seeing the sun come up over the horse farm across from our house. It's always a beautiful sight, and one I hope I'll never take for granted. It reminds me that God is who He says He is. As I see the sun rising up into the sky He painted that morning, there's something else in my line of sight: a water tower. Over the years, I've thought a lot about that water tower, and I want to use this verse to apply a principle I've learned from my thoughts about that tower.

My neighbors may think I'm an odd bird from time to time, but there's one thing I've never done. I've never yelled to them, "Hey neighbor, bring me some water from that tower so I won't have to go there and get it!" You see, I know better than that. We have city water coming right to our house, so I don't have to do a thing but turn on a faucet to bring it over.

God's perspective is a wonderful and powerful thing. The Samaritan Woman had a mistaken perspective at the time she commented on Jesus' offer of the Living Water. Like many people, she may have thought, "If I receive Christ, my life will be easy." Today, some pastors and writers teach "prosperity theology" that if we believe—*really* believe—in Jesus, then He will take away every problem and make us wealthy and happy. Wow, I wish that were true, but the Bible says that God's purposes are far higher and deeper than our happiness. When Jesus offered our Water Woman "Living Water," she wasn't thinking in spiritual terms. Instead, she thought that if she got this Living Water, it would save her a trip to the well on a daily basis. All the heavy lifting, time, and effort would be eliminated. She may have connected Jesus' promise with her spiritual thirst, but her statement in verse 11 makes me believe she was only thinking of actual water. Many of us think often of our physical needs, but we ignore our spiritual needs.

The woman was right about one point, though. Jesus' promise implied something constant and continual. When we receive the gift of Living Water, Jesus Christ, we want to continue coming back for more. The moment we accept Christ into our hearts, He lives within us, giving us that faucet handle of access to His throne. A little drop will amaze us, but through tasting that drop, we ultimately want more of Him. The truth is that His gift is sufficient, whole, and huge, but we can only take in one drop at a time. Jesus never holds back, and His blessings are in such abundance that I only need more faith to receive them. But His blessings often come disguised in trials, sufferings, mundane or mindless jobs, and other struggles. Oh yes, I believe in God's miraculous healing powers, and have seen them for myself, but every person that was ever healed later died! Without suffering, many of us wouldn't see our need for God. Jesus' grace came to us through His suffering on the Cross. In turn, we receive His Living Water gifts of love, joy, peace, patience, kindness, goodness, faithfulness, gentleness, and self-control, through our brokenness.

The Woman of the Well helps us understand that this Living Water was offered in spite of her sinfulness, but she was willing to drink of that Living Water because of her brokenness. Jesus knew her story before He met her that day, and as they talked, she began to learn the truth about the Messiah and herself. The results? I truly believe that as she sensed Jesus' love, she loved herself for the very first time that day when she left the well. Now think about this: If that were the case, wouldn't she be looking forward to her next trip back there because she fell in love with a Man who filled the aching hole in her heart and loved her perfectly? I'm sure she longed to meet him again.

My own brokenness always causes me to seek God more. My trials (or the trials of others) cause me to thirst for His deliverance. Suffering causes me to pray for the fountain of comfort and healing. Emotional trauma or grief sometimes causes me to ask others to drench me in prayer when I can't pray for myself. Sometimes an ungrateful attitude, thought, or word causes me to remember how much I need His cup of forgiveness. Water always flows downward. Whether you are high on the mountain or in the valley below, Jesus' Living Water can reach you today. He wants you to come to the Well and drink deeply and often.

Examine your perspective today. Jeremiah 17:9 says, "The heart is deceitful above all things." But the Lord searches our hearts and makes our paths straight to the Well. Christ has risen and stands ready and willing to meet our every need and to wash away every sin so that we, too, can live in freedom. Jesus was preparing her to honestly face the truth, and she was beginning to embrace her spiritual thirst. Jesus came not to take away challenges, but to change us from the inside out. In this verse, the woman was asking Jesus to bring her the Living Water, even though her perception was a little murky. That's progress, wouldn't you say?

## *Drink the Living Water*

"In the same way, after supper He took the cup, saying, 'This cup is the new covenant in my blood; do this, whenever you drink it, in remembrance of me.'" [1 Corinthians 11:25-26]

"He has delivered us from such a deadly peril, and He will deliver us. On Him we have set our hope that He will continue to deliver us, as you help us by your prayers." [2 Corinthians 1:10]

"Consider it pure joy, my brothers, whenever you face trials of many kinds, because you know that the testing of your faith develops perseverance." [James 1:2]

## *Deeper Reflections*

— Have you ever been exposed to the teaching of prosperity theology that the Christian life is just a bed of roses? If so, what impact did it have on your faith?

— Do you have hardships in your life today? What are they?

— How can the Living Water help you through the tough times?

## *Drenched in Prayer*

*Sir, give me this water that satisfies my spiritual thirst, and make me want to keep coming back for more! But even more than Your blessings and gifts, I want an honest heart to receive them. Show me the way through my present hardships or upcoming trials with grace. Amen.*

# *Letting Go*

*He told her, "Go, call your husband and come back."* [ John 4:16 ]

uch! Did Jesus have to say that? I mean, really…things were going pretty smoothly up to that point. Why did Jesus have to get so personal? I can imagine that our Samaritan Woman literally felt like going back to bed, jumping in it, and pulling the covers over her head. I know I would.

To be honest with you; I have been anxiously awaiting the day that we approached this verse, because it catapults us into the next scene of the story. Up until this point, Jesus has been extending an invitation, and our Samaritan Woman has been deciding whether or not to trust Him. The two of them have been playing a game of cat and mouse between physical thirst and spiritual thirst. He has been motivating her, nudging her ever so slightly, helping her to embrace her thirst, and daring her to move ahead. Obviously, Jesus knows her heart's desire is to proceed. Then He raises the stakes of the interaction with His directives: "Go…call…and come back."

Think about it. One second He's talking about water and giving her an invitation to quench her thirst for a lifetime, and the next minute He's getting right into the nitty-gritty of her personal life! Jesus: the private eye! How dare He? In the first part of the interaction, Jesus gave her the eternal plan. In the second part, He explained how she could experience it. He told her, in essence, that she would have to let go of her past to grab on to the promise of eternal life. *You can't continue to do the same things and expect different results.* He was directly inviting her to let go of her past and move forward with Him, but to let go of it, she first had to be bluntly honest about it. She had to acknowledge the pain and the truth of her past for the Living Truth to set her free! There can be no falsehood or deceit or denial when we encounter Truth in Person. John 14:6 says: "Jesus is the way, the *truth,* and the life."

Let's get one thing straight: I don't believe Jesus asked her to go back and retrieve her lover because He actually wanted to meet him! (But I suppose that would have made for a really intriguing conversation!) He wanted her to let go of the pain of her past relationships, where she had looked for love in all the wrong places and on all the wrong faces. The choice, though, would be hers. Jesus, the gentleman that He is, wanted her to remember the past, and come back and sit down and have a little fireside chat (or in this case, a Well-side chat) with Him. He did not desire to shame her, but rather to set her free from the pain of those past relationship and to prepare her for an intimate relationship with Him, without stain or wrinkle. In other words, He wanted to prepare His bride for worship. Here comes the Bride, all dressed in white!

When we think about letting go of our pasts, it often involves a deep and painful sense of loss, such as:

- the loss of affection or respect from a loved one who made us angry,
- the loss of a job that left us bitter,
- the loss of a wayward child who left us feeling guilty,
- the loss of self-esteem from abuse,
- the loss of a child due to abortion,
- the loss of a physical part of ourselves due to a handicap or illness that has left us depressed,
- the loss of a spouse due to a divorce which may have left us hard and cynical, or
- the loss of finances due to an accident, fire, drop in the stock market, or just plain bad budgeting that has left us despairing.

Perhaps you've experienced shame or guilt from a sinful past. Many of us need to let go of sinful behaviors such as eating disorders, alcohol, drugs, pornography, affairs, overspending, gossip, bad attitudes, and the list of struggles goes on and on… The truth is that we can't go back and relive our past, but our past can destroy our present and future if we allow it to. We have to let go of it. If we desire to be filled with the Gushing Springs of Living Water, we have to be willing to give the Spirit more of ourselves and obey Him by taking steps of faith. Water can't fill an already filled vessel. We must decrease so He can increase. *Don't think of it as getting more of the Holy Spirit, but rather, think of it as giving Him more of yourself.*

Jesus goes right for the gnawing pain the woman brought to the well. Her empty water pots were a symbol of her life. Her pain was in the form of rejection, shame, isolation, guilt, and feeling unloved. She was a social outcast. But never fear, for God is here!

Our Private Eye is also a Great Physician, and He is about to perform heart surgery at the Well. Ezekiel 26:36 says "I will give you a new heart and put a new spirit in you; I will remove from you your heart of stone and give you a heart of flesh." We must be released of the old in order to be restored with the new! Jesus goes right for the root of the problem. He knows that His Well of cleansing goes deep, and just a sprinkling has never totally revived anyone (though it might get you through the day).

This verse begins the delicate surgery of removing the old to make room for the new. The only instruments needed are Jesus' tender love, forgiveness, mercy, and grace—and her obedience in faith. One touch from the Master, one healing Word, and the crusty heart that is barren and thirsty begins to melt in the warmth of love and truth. Jesus brings life not death, peace not chaos, and rest not busyness. Ah…His Water is so good, and His bottomless Well never runs dry.

Do you see why I was awaiting this verse? Jesus is the Private Eye; He already knows what you and I try to hide, and what we think we have done so well at keeping secret. My hope today is you will be open to letting go, by answering His call of "Go, call your _____ and come back," whatever it may be.

I'll leave you today with one of my favorite little sayings that some-one gave me a while back called "Let go and Let God."

Just as a tearful child would bring a broken toy to us to mend,
so, too, I brought my fears to God because He was my friend.
But then instead of leaving Him in peace, to work alone,
I hung around and tried to help, with ways that were my own.
At last I snatched them back and cried, "How can you be so slow?"
"My child" He said, "What could I do? You never did let go?"

## Drink the Living Water

"Therefore, if anyone is in Christ, he is a new creation; the old has gone, the new has come! All this is from God, who reconciled us to himself through Christ and gave us the ministry of reconciliation: that God was reconciling the world to himself in Christ not counting men's sins against them." [2 Corinthians 5:17-19]

"Therefore, since through God's mercy we have this ministry, we do not lose heart. Rather, we have renounced secret and shameful ways; we do not use deception, nor do we distort the Word of God. On the contrary, by setting forth the truth plainly we commend ourselves to every man's conscience in the sight of God." [2 Corinthians 4:1-2]

"Husbands love your wives, just as Christ loved the church and gave himself up for her to make her holy, cleansing her by the washing with water through the word, and to present her to himself as a radiant church, without stain or wrinkle or any other blemish, but holy and blameless." [Ephesians 5:25-27]

## Deeper Reflections

— What loss have you experienced that you need to release? What does it mean to grieve that loss?

— What sin do you need to let go of today? How will your life be different when you experience God's cleansing forgiveness?

— If Jesus talked to you today, what would He ask you to go back, call upon, and come back with?

— Is fear a problem for you? Explain your answer.

— What area or areas of your life need healing and restoration?

## *Drenched in Prayer*

*Lord, You are my Shepherd, forgive me for hiding. Ever since Adam and Eve hid in the garden, the rest of us have been hiding from our sins, too. Letting go of what we are familiar with makes us feel vulnerable and open for rejection, but You never rejected the Woman at the Well. You encouraged her to be honest and open so You could heal her wounds and past hurts. I want to be whole, so please help me today. Give me the courage and grace it takes to be totally truthful with You, for I know that the truth will set me free in Your Name through the blood of Christ. Amen.*

# Receiving the Truth of Forgiveness

*"I have no husband," she replied. Jesus said to her, "You are right when you say you have no husband."* [ John 4:17 ]

This is really something! Just a minute ago, Jesus told the woman to call her husband, and now He tells her, "You are right when you say you have no husband." Why do you suppose He asked her to go call a husband He knew she didn't have? (You've gotta love this story!)

Perhaps Jesus wanted to see if she would tell the truth? (He, of course, already knew the truth.) Perhaps He just wanted to see if she would even respond. A response would be a step in the right direction in her acceptance of His previous invitation to pour out the Living Water for her. Let's think about this for a moment: If she hadn't wanted to accept Jesus' invitation, she could have walked away at this point rather than talking any more with Him. It would have been so easy for her to say, "Have a nice day. Goodbye. See you later." and walk back to town. But she didn't. She made the wise choice to respond to Jesus with honesty.

A response is required when accepting a gift. Many people have a hard time receiving gifts, because to accept a gift in the form of "help" makes us feel that we aren't able to handle it on our own—and that hurts our pride. A dear friend taught me: To receive a gift actually blesses the giver. The Woman at the Well was actually beginning to bless Jesus, as strange as that may sound, just by interacting with Him. Her honesty was a sign of her acceptance to move forward.

There are three things required in order to receive God's gift. The three D's are:

- A *determination* that you need it,
- A *desire* to have it, and
- A *decision* to accept it.


Our Samaritan Woman covers all three D's before she leaves the Well that day. In this interchange, the Samaritan Woman and Jesus were on the same playing field of honesty. The chitchat, surface conversation was over, and they are now dipping below the surface for some real water! Jesus is in effect saying, "You've been truthful. You haven't tried to blame, complain, judge, take revenge on, or question my challenge for you to call your husband." The soil of *forgiveness* is being cultivated as they speak. Sometimes we love peace rather than truth, and we tend to isolate rather than infiltrate. But truth and grace go hand in hand in Kingdom work.

Let's dip our buckets into the Well of forgiveness and examine a few truths today:

- Biblical forgiveness doesn't *ignore or deny* the wrong.
- Biblical forgiveness transfers the responsibility to pay for *spiritual and emotional* debts to Jesus.
- Biblical forgiveness requires *trust and faith* in Jesus' sacrifice for *our own sins and the sins of others.*
- Biblical forgiveness releases *resentments and bitterness* so that we can begin to receive *restoration and transformation.*
- Biblical forgiveness keeps no *record or tally* of *wrongs or hurts.*
- Biblical forgiveness is a choice we make out of *love and obedience* for Christ.
- Biblical forgiveness is accomplished *through and in Christ Jesus.*

Personally, the hardest person I have ever had to forgive was myself for my stupid choices that hurt those I love. But when I realized why I needed to forgive myself—because Christ died for me so that I could and would forgive myself—I knew it was the first step toward lasting peace and joy. To avoid forgiving myself out of selfish pride was to deny Him and what He stands for.

The second hardest person I have ever had to forgive was my little sister who committed suicide. But then, to not forgive her would have in fact been a slow death for me. I firmly believe Christ is in the business of suicide prevention through forgiveness. After my sister's death, I realized how much I had in common with the Woman at the Well. Both of us dealt with similar issues of rejection, guilt, and betrayal— just in a different set of circumstances. Perhaps you can relate, too.

Remember how I said to receive a gift blesses the giver? I suppose the best blessing we can give Christ is to receive His gift of forgiveness for our own sins, and then to offer that same gift of forgiveness to others as a sign of our acceptance and blessing to Him. Through the gift of forgiveness, we can begin to have the intimacy, personal relationship, and Living Water Christ wants us to enjoy. We must first be released of past hurts that continue to drag us down, shackles of fear that bind our souls, emotional debts, wrong thinking, negative behavior patterns, and bitterness. Then and only then, through forgiveness we begin to cross over from death to life.

Speaking of life, did you know I was physically born on 4-17, April 17th? (Forget the year, gifts are welcome!) The same numbers of today's verse...and not only that, but it was *Easter Sunday,* the day of resurrection and ascension into heaven of our Lord Jesus Christ! To me this is proof positive that transformation is possible and forgiveness is absolutely necessary in order to experience the resurrection of ourselves as new creations! God has a plan and purpose for each of us.

I love you all, and I pray God will do a mighty work in your spirit today. Embrace your thirst and empty your well of self for the transforming power of the Living Water!

## Drink the Living Water

"The thief comes only to steal and kill and destroy; I have come that they may have life, and have it to the full." [John 10:10]

"The Word became flesh and made his dwelling among us. We have seen his glory, the glory of the One and only, who came from the Father, full of grace and truth." [John 1:14]

"If you, O Lord, kept a record of sins, O Lord, who could stand? But with You there is forgiveness; therefore You are feared." [Psalm 130:3-4]

"On that day a fountain will be opened to the house of David and the inhabitants of Jerusalem, to cleanse them from sin and impurity." [Zechariah 13:1]

## Deeper Reflections

— What are some reasons that facing the pains of the past are so difficult? What are some things we fear in facing them?

— Today, will you harbor the hurt or welcome the healing? Explain your answer.

— Describe some of the blessings of knowing we are forgiven.

— List those people you still need to forgive, and what their offense was.

— Is there anything you have done that you still need to forgive yourself for? If so, what?

— Pray the prayer below for all those the Holy Spirit has brought to mind.

## *Drenched in Prayer*

Here is a prayer of forgiveness you may want to pray today for yourself, or others:

*Father, I thank You for the divine opportunity to forgive. Today, Lord, You alone are the Judge. I do not have Your perspective, and I do not understand why_____ (name of person) did this or said this to me. However, I have made the decision to let go of them and their actions and words. I give it to You, and I forgive _____ (name of person) for _____ _____ (state offense and be as specific as you need to). I forgive him/her for taking the peace from me that you died for me to enjoy. I choose by Your grace to forgive, and I won't ever again hold this against him/her. And Lord, I ask now that You heal me of all that has been stolen from me through these circumstances. Restore and transform me physically, emotionally, and spiritually. Show me who I am in Christ. Thank You for the complete assurance of Your justice and mercy for all those involved, including myself. In Jesus' name, Amen. (Repeat this prayer for each offender).*

# Forgiveness Then Healing

*"The fact is, you have had five husbands, and
the man you now have is not your husband.
What you have just said is quite true."*

[ John 4:18 ]

In the previous verses, Jesus told the Samaritan Woman to go get her husband and come back, and then she replied honestly, "I have no husband." These verses hit a soft spot in my heart. A widow is a woman whose husband has died, but a woman whose husband has divorced her could also be considered a widow because the relationship died. It may have died physically, spiritually, or emotionally. I'm not making a theological statement here, but I want to point out that many divorced women feel like widows, alone and discarded. I feel so sorry for single moms whose husbands walked out on them, whatever the circumstances. God calls us to exhibit faultless and pure "religion" in taking care of "widows and orphans" (see James

1:27). When we give to those less fortunate without desiring anything in return, we serve as Christ served and we love as Christ loved.

In this passage, Jesus was practicing what He preaches in His Word. He was about to take care of this woman who had lost five husbands from what could have been divorce or death—we don't know. Even more astonishing, He didn't ask her for money, to sign up for the casserole committee, work in the nursery, or even to follow a set of religious rules. He didn't remind her of her sordid past, but instead, He cleansed her of it. He didn't hound her about her bad reputation, but he gave her a new reputation that would do away with her fears, doubts, and sin. He offered her restoration, redemption, and relationship. She'd have to be a fool to pass that up, don't you agree?

So, we're back to the issue of forgiveness. Our perspective on forgiveness tremendously affects our relationships. There are a few misconceptions about forgiveness that are worth pointing out, because the *real* benefits of forgiveness far outweigh the *perceived* benefits of hanging on to unforgiveness. The truth is that Jesus "hung on the tree" for that very reason—so we would accept His forgiveness for ourselves, be reconciled to Him, and offer this forgiveness to others.

I like to call these myths of forgiveness "leaks in our spiritual wells," because they truly cause our spiritual tanks to run dry.

## *Leaks in our Spiritual Wells*

- **Leak #1:** To forgive is to be weak.
  Wrong! Jesus forgave others at His point of greatest weakness on the cross of Calvary in order to show His ultimate strength and power.
- **Leak #2:** To forgive is to lose control.
  Wrong again! The person unwilling to forgive has no control worth having! Because any control apart from God's control will

only lead us down the empty well of bitterness, anger, and resentment, keeping us in a prison of our own making. Have you ever seen a prison inmate in control of his or her own life?

- **Leak #3:** To forgive sets me up for further hurt.

  That's sometimes true, but how would you rather live: closed down, walled in, pent up, and alone, or open to help others, honest and vulnerable, discerning, and free in the Spirit? Unfortunately, hurt is part of the world we live in. If we try to protect ourselves too much, we can't have rich, real, vulnerable relationships. It's a risk, but it's a risk worth taking.

- **Leak #4:** People need to pay for how they hurt me.

  No, they don't! Actually, Jesus took the punishment for our sins and theirs, but this fact shouldn't be as a license to sin! (See Romans 6:1-2.) Accountability is essential, along with grace and truth, in order to see God's glory (John 1:14).

- **Leak #5:** If I just ignore it, (the forgiveness issue) it will go away.

  No, it won't! This may be the biggest lie ever. Do you know where explosions of anger come from? School shootings, family murders, drug overdoses, sexual assaults…or more commonly, name calling, bitterness, anger, and walls of self-protection are the results of people ignoring hurts and hoping the pain would go away. Do you know what happens to unforgiveness? Eventually, it can eat us alive and turn into depression. The old saying comes to mind: *"To look within is to be depressed; to look up is to be impressed."*

In this passage, our Well Woman comes to terms of endearment with Jesus through terms of forgiveness with herself and others. The truth sets her free, without begging, without condemnation, without guilt, but only through the unique, transforming and sustaining love of God.

Now consider these verses that complement our story so well. Mark told a story about four men bringing a friend to Jesus. They encountered obstacles, but nothing could stop them. "Since they could not get to Jesus because of the crowd, they made an opening in the roof above Jesus and after digging through it, lowered the mat the paralyzed man was lying on. When Jesus saw their faith, he said to the paralytic, 'Son, your sins are forgiven' " (Mark 2:4-5).

In this story, four men bring their paralytic friend to Jesus for healing. Their faith was so strong that they even dropped him through the roof where Jesus was teaching. Oh, that we might pursue Jesus like this! I believe this passage of Scripture gives us some real insight into God's kingdom practices. Jesus said to the paralyzed man, "Son, your sins are forgiven."

That's odd, don't you think? The four men didn't bring their friend for forgiveness. They brought him for healing, but Jesus gave the paralytic what He knows is needed before the healing can take place—just like He was doing with the Samaritan Woman. Healing often follows forgiveness in heaven's order of things.

Many times we try to do it in reverse. "Heal me, Jesus, then I'll follow you. My way first, then Yours," we bargain. We don't need to live in despair, because His intentions are always best for His children. Peace doesn't come from asking Him to do what we want and then expecting Him to bless our request. On the contrary! It comes from connecting with Him on a daily basis and following His plan, not our own. His priority is to reform our inner world first. God's thoughts and ways are always much higher and deeper than ours, and we will never understand it all. But one thing is for sure: His life was spent to extend forgiveness in order to facilitate healing and transformation on the inside of us first. Glory be to God!

## Drink the Living Water

"You, therefore, have no excuse, you who pass judgment on someone else, for at whatever point you judge the other, you are condemning yourself, because you who pass judgment do the same things." [Romans 2:1]

"Therefore, there is now no condemnation for those who are in Christ Jesus, because through Christ Jesus the law of the Spirit of life set me free from the law of sin and death." [Romans 8:1-2]

"Bear with each other and forgive whatever grievances you may have against one another. Forgive as the Lord forgave you." [Colossians 3:13]

## Deeper Reflections

— Review the "leaks" in this lesson. Which one do you most often fall into? How does it affect your heart and your relationships?

— How would you connect unforgiveness and depression? What are some other consequences of harboring bitterness in our hearts?

— Read Ephesians 4:32. What is the connection between our experience of Christ's forgiveness and our ability to forgive others?

— Are you on your way to becoming a Woman of the Well, healed and restored? Explain your answer.

## *Drenched in Prayer*

*Lord, I want to be a Woman of the Well, healed and restored. Transform my heart; turn it inside out and upside down if You must. I don't just want to look good on the outside. I want my insides to radiate Your love and mercy so others are drawn to You. Make me a Woman of the Well as I seek to obey You by receiving Your forgiveness today and trusting You to guard my heart. Amen.*

# Do You See What I See?

*"Sir," the woman said, "I can see that you are a prophet."* [ John 4:19 ]

don't know about you, but when someone I don't know gets too personal too quickly, I'm a bit apprehensive! Jesus had just gotten pretty personal with His reminder of the Samaritan Woman's five husbands. At this point, our woman does what most women who have developed a sense of self-protection do—she changes the subject. (You've got to love this. When women feel uncomfortable, we can change the conversation in a split second!) Instead of talking more about herself, she shifted the focus to Jesus. Smart woman, this gal, and a quick thinker. She could tell that this Man wasn't an ordinary guy. She believed he was "a prophet," but in fact, He was "The Prophet."

When she made the statement about Jesus being a prophet, she may have been a bit flustered by the interaction, possibly blushing from the embarrassment at Jesus knowing her intimate life history and anxious that He had exposed her dirty little secrets. To deflect attention and change the subject, she shifted from *personal relationships* to *religion*. She wanted to keep it light and comfortable!

This above analysis of the passage is very common among Bible teachers and commentaries, but I think there may have been another explanation for her statement. Are you ready? I believe the woman knows *exactly* who Jesus is. She has seen the loving look in his eyes, and she can tell this man is the promised Messiah. She has met her Maker, and she knows it. Her statement, then, is simply stating the obvious. I mean…*hello*…Jesus is standing right in front of her! Let's give her a little credit. She had to develop some savvy and grit to survive. In a culture that gives divorced women no breaks at all, she has persevered by her wits and determination.

Her statement about Jesus being a prophet may have signaled that she believed He was delivering a divine message from God, or it may signify that she believed He was the Messiah and Savior foretold by Isaiah. So, was she changing the subject, or was she actually digging deeper into the Well of Living Water? Go ahead and decide for yourself. In Matthew 5:8, Jesus said, "Blessed are the pure in heart, for they will see God." The woman's heart may have been prepared and pure, through forgiveness of sins, so that she recognized Jesus as God.

John provides us with enough of the conversation between Jesus and the woman to fill us in on the essentials of their relationship, but the two probably had a much fuller interaction than John relates. The point is that Jesus pursued a person others rejected, and she responded with questions, and eventually, faith. Her honesty and boldness draw us to her. When we encounter Jesus, we can be bold, too. When we see who Jesus is and come to know Him personally, there is a bubbling, a pouring out of boldness that we can't prevent. What would the world be like if more people bubbled over with this passion for telling who Jesus is!

## Drink the Living Water

"Create in me a pure heart, O God." [Psalm 51:10]

"Blessed are those who hunger and thirst for righteousness, for they will be filled." [Matthew 5:6]

"After they prayed, the place where they were meeting was shaken. And they were all filled with the Holy Spirit and spoke the word of God boldly." [Acts 4:31]

## Deeper Reflections

— Do you think the woman used her statement about Jesus being a prophet to deflect conversation from herself, or do you think she really understood that Jesus was The Prophet? Explain your answer.

— Is boldness just a personality trait, or can anyone be bold? In your answer, describe how different types of people show their boldness in different ways.

— On a scale of 0 (not at all) to 10 (the max), rate your level of boldness to pursue Christ and tell others about Him. Does your level of boldness need to change? Explain your response.

## *Drenched in Prayer*

*Creator God, Create in me a pure heart, and help me to see You clearly, love You dearly, and follow You nearly. Amen.*

# The Worship and the Declaration

# Believe Me, Woman!

*Jesus declared, "Believe me, woman, a time is coming when you will worship the Father neither on this mountain nor in Jerusalem."*

[ John 4:21 ]

Don't you wish you could have heard the tone of Jesus' voice when He spoke these words? When we see His statement written in black and white, it's easy to think of Him being angry or frustrated when He uses the term "woman," but that's not the case at all. He was being kind, gracious, and compassionate. I can almost see a smile on His face as He spoke those words. The word "woman" in this verse is translated in Greek as *gune*, which refers specifically to a wife. Jesus was calling the Samaritan Woman His wife! Go back and read it again imagining Jesus' tone of voice filled with kindness.

Jesus began this statement with an encouragement for the woman to believe Him. He says the same thing to you and me today. And He has proven that He is supremely, completely, and wonderfully trustworthy! Why then, are we so hesitant to believe Him? Instead…

We fail to believe God has chosen us,

therefore we don't seek or search for our Savior.

We fail to believe God has given us royal robes to wear,

therefore we walk around in rags of deprivation.

We fail to believe God loves us,

therefore we don't obey His instructions.

We fail to believe God has a plan and a future for us,

therefore we never fulfill our purpose.

We fail to believe God's faithfulness stands firm,

therefore we dive into despair.

We fail to believe God answers our prayers,

therefore we just don't ask.

We fail to believe God's truth sets us free,

therefore we keep living in bondage to lies.

We fail to believe God's shield of protection,

therefore we fret in fear.

We fail to believe God promises to provide,

therefore we work like maniacs to provide for ourselves.

We fail to believe God's warnings and discipline,

therefore we continue in sin, refusing to repent.

We fail to believe in God's mercy and forgiveness,

therefore we continue to waste away in self-condemnation.

We fail to believe God's compassion is new every morning,

therefore we fail to meet Him for quiet time.

We fail to believe God's resurrection healing power,
therefore we never find wholeness or restoration.
We fail to believe God brings joy in the morning,
therefore we mourn our losses for the rest of our days.
We fail to believe God has the answers for our questions,
therefore we never ask for wisdom.
We fail to believe God's plan cannot be thwarted,
therefore we won't wait for Him or trust in His timing.
We fail to believe God can give us rest,
therefore we are disquieted and burdened by all kinds of
stresses.
We fail to believe God can crown us with beauty,
therefore our lives remain in ashes.
We fail to believe God wants us to consider others better than
ourselves,
therefore we put progress before people.
We fail to believe God can cleanse our hearts and consciences,
therefore we are oppressed by guilt and shame.
We fail to believe in the Messiah's offer of Living Water,
therefore our souls remain thirsty.
We fail to believe God wants a personal relationship with us,
therefore we walk in loneliness.
We fail to believe God sent His Son to die for our sins
and that He promises us eternal life,
therefore we forfeit all the blessings, plans, life and power of
the resurrected Christ.

## Drink the Living Water

"See to it brothers, that none of you has a sinful, unbelieving heart that turns away from the living God. But encourage one another daily." [Hebrews 3:12-13]

"Jesus said to her, 'I am the resurrection and the life. He who believes in me will live, even though he dies; and whoever lives and believes in me will never die. Do you believe this?'" [John 11:25]

"Then Jesus said, 'Did I not tell you that if you believed, you would see the glory of God?'" [John 11:40]

"If anyone is thirsty, let him come to me and drink. Whoever believes in me, as the Scripture has said, streams of living water will flow from within him." [John 7:37-38]

"Having believed, you were marked in him with a seal, the promised Holy Spirit, who is a deposit guaranteeing our inheritance until the redemption of those who are God's possession—to the praise of his glory." [Ephesians 1:13-14]

## Deeper Reflections

— What difference does it mean to you to read today's passage with the thought of Jesus being kind and compassionate instead of frustrated with the woman?

— As you read the statements of unbelief in this lesson, which ones stood out to you because you struggle with them?

— What would it mean in your heart and your experience for you to trust God more in these areas?

— Are you encouraging your family and neighbors and friends with the Truth? —Are you encouraged by God's Truth today?

— What are some specific things Jesus wants you to believe Him for today?

## Drenched in Prayer

*Lord, I remember the story where the man said to Jesus, "I believe, help me overcome my unbelief!" That's my prayer today, "I believe, but help me overcome my unbelief!" Infuse me with faith today through Your utter faithfulness, mercy and love for me. Amen.*

# The Decision

*"Our fathers worshiped on this mountain, but you Jews claim that the place where we must worship is in Jerusalem." Jesus declared... "You Samaritans worship what you do not know; we worship what we do know, for salvation is from the Jews."* [ John 4:20, 22 ]

My married name is Lovett, as in "Love it or leave it!" At this point in the conversation, I believe the Samaritan Woman was deciding if she loved Jesus or not. To be honest, it's been a very awkward conversation. A total stranger knows everything about her! And yet there's something in His eyes and His voice that tells her this man is different. Everything in her says to run away, but she decides to stay and engage Him in conversation. Still, she doesn't understand what He's offering her. She still thinks spiritual life is about places, not the Person. But Jesus is standing right in front of her! The puzzle pieces are slowly coming together.

We are entering into scene three of our story, moving from initiation of the relationship to the freedom of forgiveness and now into true worship. Allow me to paraphrase these verses for us today: "My father goes to the Church of Christ on Main Street, but you say you go to the Church of Grace, on Second Street—what gives? Where should I go to worship God?"

Jesus replies, "I can help you. I can show you the truth!"

Our Samaritan Woman is now shifting her paradigm from "so many men and so little time," to finding the right kind of church! At this moment, she's reaching out to Jesus, but she's confused about the next step to take. Through her fresh encounter with the Living God, she has been restored, transformed, and healed. Now she wants an answer to the pressing question: "Where can I go to find You when You leave?"

Oh my! Can it be? She's falling in love again! Only this time, it's different. This time she's at ease, not feeling ashamed or guilty, because she has been purified and cleansed. This time she feels genuine love for the very first time. Jesus has met her at her deepest point of despair. She has finally met a love that will never abandon her.

Jesus is now her seventh husband, counting the five divorces and the one common law marriage with the man she has been living with. But now she is leaving behind her painful past, which damaged and disappointed her, and she is beginning a real relationship.

By the way, don't you find it astonishing that the number seven represents wholeness in the Bible! Our Water Woman is now not only a Well Woman, but she also becomes a symbol for the completed, restored Bride of Christ. She is the representation of purity with her husband, Jesus, and the fulfillment of the intimate relationship we are meant to have.

But our adversary, Satan, doesn't want us to have a personal relationship with God. As the day of the Lord's return comes closer, the evil forces around us will increase to spread doubt and fear, chaos and destruction. The enemy of our souls will try to do whatever it takes to hinder our relationship with God. His only rule is: whatever works. He will sow confusion and make it seem difficult for us to find God, just like the confusion the Samaritan Woman experienced. We all need to be on guard, and to look at confusion as a ploy to keep our focus away from the Almighty God who brings peace, love, and joy. Every day brings temptations and pressures. We need to be alert, on guard, and ready with the sword of the Spirit, the truth of God's Word.

I want to draw a parallel between the Woman at the Well and the experience of some of us today. People are still preoccupied with the place of worship rather than the Person we worship. Many people are "church hopping," looking for the perfect church or a pastor who entertains them more than any other. When we are distracted by these pursuits, we have a part-time lover rather than a full-time Lord. Could it be that we're not so different from the Samaritan Woman, indecisive about where to find God? Could it be He is right in front of us? We need to ask God for wisdom to examine our hearts, and we need Him to give us courage to repent if that's needed.

Jesus warned His disciples: "Watch out that no one deceives you. Many will come in my name, claiming, 'I am he,' and [they] will deceive many. When you hear of wars and rumors of wars, do not be alarmed. Such things must happen, but the end is still to come. Nation will rise against nation, and kingdom against kingdom. There will be earthquakes in various places, and famines. These are the beginning of birth pains. *You must be on your guard.*" (Mark 13:5-9, italics mine.)

When we read the newspaper or watch the evening news, we see that evil has increased all around us. Shootings are common, false religions and cults are popular, sexual predators are preying on our children, chat-room stalkers are on the loose, nations war against nations, the threat of terrorism faces us daily, and we experience many health concerns and financial problems. Satan is becoming bolder because he knows his time is short. While the enemy is prowling around like a lion ready to devour us, are we on guard? Our Samaritan Woman may have been caught off guard by Jesus' questions, but she was open to His correction. Her humble, open heart was the key to her response to Him. I hope you and I are just as open to Jesus today.

We guard ourselves from biting insects with bug spray, from the sun with sunscreen, from poverty with insurance, from relationship problems with isolation, from authenticity with masks, and from intruders with high-tech security cameras and systems. We attempt to guard ourselves from criticism by trying to be perfect, from starvation with overindulgence, from illness with drugs, from boredom with pleasure, from intimacy with distance, and from the truth with lies. We have leaf guards on our gutters, armed guards at our malls, air marshals in our planes, gas masks for biochemical warfare, and even guard dogs in our yards. Regardless of how important some of these may be to us, they should not be the focus of our lives. Don't be misled; our future is only secure with Jesus Christ.

In his book, *Breakthrough Prayer*,[1] Jim Cymbala asks, "What does it matter how well we know the Bible if we don't aggressively love the folks Christ died for? What good are the gifts of the Spirit if they're only for people like us—people we feel comfortable with? Is this Christianity? Is it found anywhere in the Bible? The greatest deception of all has nothing to do with New Age philosophy or the occult. Rather, it is the idea that we can represent and preach Christ while being strangers to his heart of love."

Christ crossed all barriers of racial and economic prejudices in order to reach the Woman at the Well, and it prompted her to ask Him, "Where can I find this type of love?" Many people look at today's fractured and superficial churches, and they ask the same question, "Where can I go to find Christ?"

---

1   Jim Cymbala, *Breakthrough Prayer*, Zondervan Publishers, Grand Rapids, MI, Copyright 2003, pg. 121

Today, let's engage Jesus with questions. We may be confused, and we may need Him to correct our thinking, but let's be like our Well Woman and ask questions without fear. Let's drink deeply from His Well, loving every minute, not leaving until we are drenched in His goodness, grace, and assurance. Then and only then can we love like He loves and be certain of His unending love that will never leave us! Have you decided to follow Jesus yet?

## *Drink the Living Water*
"You must be on your guard." [Mark 13:9]

"No one knows about that day or hour, not even the angels in heaven, nor the Son, but only the Father. Be on guard! Be alert! You do not know when that time will come." [Mark 13:32-33]

"Yet I hold this against you: You have forsaken your first love." [Revelation 2:4]

"Never will I leave you; never will I forsake you." [Hebrews 13:5]

"Guard your steps when you go to the house of God." [Ecclesiastes 5:1]

## *Deeper Reflections*
— What do you look for in a church family? Be honest. Do you really look for God, or are you there to be entertained? Explain your answer.


— What would it mean for you to really find God in a local church congregation? How would it affect your sense of community, purpose, and love for people there?

— Do you have times when you think God has left you and you aren't able to find Him? How do you normally respond in those situations? How do you need to respond in those situations in the future?

— How can you guard yourself from the things of the world that distract your focus from God?

— Can you say, like the Samaritan Woman, that you have decided to follow Jesus?

## *Drenched in Prayer*

*Loving Lord Jesus, in this ever-changing world, it's so difficult to balance it all. Help me to first remember You before making decisions about my future. Like the Woman at the Well, lead me to Yourself when I doubt, and help me to love You more and more each day so that I won't be tempted to put my faith in other things or people. Teach me how to guard my heart above all things, and forgive me for not taking You seriously at times. May I practice Your living presence in my life today. Amen.*

# The Appointed Time

*"Yet a time is coming and has now come when the true worshipers will worship the Father in spirit and truth, for they are the kind of worshiper the Father seeks. God is spirit, and His worshipers must worship in spirit and in truth."* [ John 4:23–24 ]

We are designed by our Creator to worship Him in Spirit and in Truth. As long as our relationship with Him is rich and real, the location of our worship doesn't matter. God doesn't reside in buildings, but in the soft, humble hearts of those who love Him. In Frances J. Roberts book, *Come Away My Beloved*,[2] she writes: "By setting your soul through deliberate choice of your will to

---

2    Frances J. Roberts, *Come Away My Beloved*, King's Farspan, Inc. Ojai, CA, 1973, pg. 83

pursue the worship of God by praying in the Spirit, thou shalt find thy faith strengthened and thy life bathed in the love of God."

Today, I want to share one of my own personal love stories with you. In 1998 God spoke *Women of the Well Ministry* into being. I had just finished my first book, *On Guard* (which you had a small taste of yesterday,) and I went to church to worship. It was a Saturday evening, so I found a service that fit my schedule. I arrived for a time of praise, and the greeter handed me the bulletin for the service. Much to my amazement, the sermon was titled, "Woman at the Well"! I was thrilled beyond measure. I had come to thank God for His goodness and faithfulness, and He had turned the tables on me with a huge surprise! What were the odds of *that* sermon being preached on *that* particular night? I had finished my book, and He confirmed my ministry! My spirit connected with His. I was overwhelmed by His love and purpose for my life, and I was set free to worship God unhindered, fully, and as extravagantly as I desired. I'll never forget that night. It felt as if God and I were the only ones in the sanctuary!

Shortly after being turned down by several publishers for that book, God spoke to me that my work to write it was only preparation for the second book! I wasn't too happy with Him that all my efforts seemed to be going to waste. He then gave me a verse out of Habakkuk, which, quite honestly, was fairly obscure to me at that point in my life. Habakkuk 2:2-3 says, "Then the Lord replied: 'Write down the revelation and make it plain on tablets so that a herald may run with it. For the revelation awaits an appointed time; it speaks of the end and will not prove false. Though it linger, wait for it; it will certainly come and will not delay.'"

At the time, this passage seemed to be a promise for my first book, but little did I know! Almost seven years later, as I sit and look at this verse and the John 4:23-24 passage for today, I can't help but see the connection. Today is the appointed time for the revelation of the Woman at the Well story: the women, the water, the worship, and the witness. God has given us women a challenge and a commission to accept God's restoration and to advance the kingdom of God with Him, in Spirit and in Truth, in these thirsty times, when it seems everyone is searching in a dry and barren land. Being "on guard" is an essential part of growing in our faith so that the enemy of our souls won't be given a firm place to stand in our lives. We need to deny him a stronghold in our hearts and close the door to the prison cell of lies in our minds. The time has come for the Bride to be purified, on guard, and blameless! God's plan and timing are perfect.

Sometime after God gave me the Habakkuk verse, I was in a Christian bookstore when a long, narrow, beautifully framed picture caught my eye. It depicted a little girl with long hair, much like my own when I was young. She was sitting in front of a huge grandfather clock, reading a lovely picture book. I knew God was speaking to me, assuring me of His promise, "awaiting an appointed time" once again. He is so creative! The passage at the bottom of the picture was Psalm 31:15: "My times are in thy hand." I knew I had to buy this picture, and as I stepped up to the check out counter, the intuitive clerk looked wide-eyed at me and exclaimed: "Oh, this is an original and is signed by the artist!" How was a girl to know? I felt as if God bought me a present that day!

God is truly intimate and knows how to speak to our hearts in a very personal way—if we will just be attentive to His Spirit.

Today I sat looking at that picture and meditating on our verse, and again I realized what a gift it is to worship our God in Spirit and in Truth. He is so awesome! Whether we worship at this church or that, He desires that our hearts live in truth as we walk in the Spirit, not the flesh. The pieces and the times of our lives are in His hands.

When we look back at the marvelous deeds He has done, and how intricately His golden strands of love for us are woven together, we will be prompted to worship Him in Spirit and Truth. We love Him for what He does for us, but His nature and character are the Well from which His actions flow. God is love!

In Greek, the word "worship" *(proskuneo)* means, "to kiss." It's an intimate act of homage or reverence to God. I think the best worship is done in solitude. When have you ever seen a truly intimate kiss in public? True worship is our way of loving God back. True worship is life changing. It is a thankful response, not a repayment for what God has done. On the other hand, praise is done through our singing that gives glory and thanks to God. Our worship is an intimate "face to face" encounter between God and us.

Many women face empty wells each day because their connection with God is far from intimate. Our praise and worship are usually experienced only in corporate church settings. Please accept today's message into your heart: God desires you to worship Him every day. He desires you to have an intimate relationship of love with Him. To worship Him you must meet Him on His terms, in His throne room, and with His truth residing in you.

The time is coming, and has now come, ladies. Are we up to the challenge? Our bigger churches, fancier sermons, fashion shows, craft days, and tea parties may be fun, but they can't convert an unsaved soul without the power of the Holy Spirit working through us. But as we seek to worship Him, are inflamed with His passion, are bubbling over with joy from the divine stream within us, we will experience the thrill of seeing Him answer our prayers, and thirsty people will flock to Him. We need this truth to settle deep in our own hearts. There are still lots of unsaved thirsty souls still on the outside of our churches looking in. What do they see?

We can worship Christ for His work on the cross for us. He died for us so that our sins would be forgiven and we could be reconciled to intimacy with Him. His greatest desire is for us to know Him. His golden strand of grace has erased our sin and granted us entry into an abundant eternity, now and forever with Him. How much better to start that relationship of knowing Him in Spirit and in Truth now, rather than later? We have come to this place for such a time as this. The appointed time has arrived!

## Drink the Living Water

"How can I repay the Lord for all his goodness to me? I will lift up the cup of salvation and call on the name of the Lord. I will fulfill my vows to the Lord in the presence of all his people." [Psalm 116:12-14]

"Be still and know that I am God." [Psalm 46:10]

"The fruit of righteousness will be peace; the effect of righteousness will be quietness and confidence forever." [Isaiah 32:17]

"For it is we who are the circumcision, we who worship by the Spirit of God, who glory in Christ Jesus, and who put no confidence in the flesh—though I myself have reasons for such confidence. But whatever was to my profit I now consider loss for the sake of Christ." [Philippians 3:3, 7]

## *Deeper Reflections*

— Do you spend more time with the busyness of religion or the stillness of a rich, real relationship with God? Explain your answer.

— What do the verses 23-24 suggest about our restoration and fulfillment in Christ?

— Has God ever made you a promise that was conditional upon waiting for His timing? If so, what was the promise, and how long did you wait, or are you still waiting?

— What are some reasons waiting is so hard for us, even when we are assured that God has our best interest at heart?

— Describe a time when you experienced intimate worship with God. Describe the attitude of your heart and how God spoke to you at that time.

— Do you lean more towards Spirit (sensing impressions from God) or Truth (focusing on God's Word) in your own worship? Is this out of balance in any way? Explain your answer.

— What names can you add to this list of names that we worship God by: Holy, Sovereign, Almighty, Loving, and Merciful? How might adding these to your prayers help you worship Him more fully?

## *Drenched in Prayer*

*Jesus, transform my soul. Teach me what it means to worship You in Spirit and in Truth. Help me to step up and be a Woman of the Well instead of a woman of the world so that I can be set apart and holy as I wait for Your return. Bring the intimacy that I desire to my relationship with You. Show me who You are. Help me use my time wisely as I listen for Your voice, and help me reach out to others in love. Thank You for being a God of compassion and mercy. I love You! Amen.*

# Faith Explained

*The woman said, "I know that Messiah"*
*(called Christ) is coming. When He comes,*
*He will explain everything to us."* [ John 4:25]

Come He has, and come back He will!

The Samaritan Woman's response to Jesus is a key phrase in our study. It puts a different light on our perception of her story. Let me explain. Many Bible teachers have taught that the story of the Woman at the Well was intended primarily to illustrate evangelism. Certainly, that's true, but I believe it was intended also for women who already believe in Jesus and know He is coming back, but they aren't living the abundant life Jesus promised. They don't have the intimate relationship that He desires so deeply for each of to have. In verse 20, she told Jesus where "her" people worshipped. I firmly believe that this is God's story of restoration for Christian women today with half empty wells—the ones that feel like there just has to be more to the Christian life than they're experiencing. How many women know Jesus, go to church, and yet, like the Samaritan Woman, keep looking elsewhere for satisfaction, security, and love? We continually drain our wells with busyness, and we fail to see or hear or receive the true revelations of God's mighty love for us in close, personal, intimate, encounters with Jesus Christ. Our insecurities and fears about ourselves and about our King confuse us! It's time we wake up, ladies, and smell the coffee!

In his book, *The Pressure's Off,*[3] author Larry Crabb wrote, " The great tragedy in modern Christianity is that pools of living water are bubbling in the burning sand of our souls and we don't know it. We haven't dug deep enough through the debris of our self-deception, through the strategies we carefully follow to make life work to drink from the divine stream within. We're drinking polluted water and thinking it's pure. Worse, we're feeling refreshed. But it's false refreshment; it's both contrived and counterfeit. It has no power to turn us into people who persevere through shattered dreams for the sake of God's pleasure and others faith. It is a sentimental temporary shallow good feelings refreshment that never dislodges self."

When we accept God's grace purely and solely as a means for "fire insurance" but fail to experience the abundant life in Christ by not exercising the spiritual disciplines and connecting with His Word, our wells remain half empty. It's like having a new Mercedes in your garage but not knowing how to drive. It sounds nice to be able to say you have it, but what good is it? In Galatians, Paul was astounded that those believers had missed the point so badly. He wrote, "After begin-

---

3    Larry Crabb, *The Pressure's Off,* Waterbrook Press, Colorado Springs, CO, 2002, pg. 42

ning with the Spirit, are you now trying to attain your goal by human effort?" You can't tell the difference between an unsaved person and one who is saved but carnal (worldly). Both try to attain peace and the abundant life through possessions, approval, or prestige. These may satisfy for a moment, but they eventually leave us empty. Who wants to drink from a well that is half-empty and stagnant? That doesn't sound too good to me! I want to drink from a Well that is overflowing, gushing with joy, peace, grace and truth! My new motto is: " Don't overwork—overflow!" Paul goes on to give a cheerleading rah-rah for those who believe in the gospel of grace by telling us to consider Abraham: "He believed God and it was credited to him as righteousness." (Galatians 3:6)

Our Samaritan Woman said she "knew" the Messiah was coming, and yet that Messiah was standing right in front of her! I wonder how many of us miss Jesus in the same way, and I wonder why that can happen so easily. The answer, I'm convinced, is that we are looking intently, but in the wrong places. We are too often focused on our fears and doubts instead of God's goodness, grace, and power. When our eyes are on the wrong things, our faith fails, and we miss Jesus. Like the woman before her encounter with Jesus, many of us don't know the God we claim to worship. And worse yet, many of us love the good feeling of worship rather than focusing on the true object of our worship: Christ Himself.

A lack of knowledge about God leads to a lack of passion for God and the absence of true worship. But a knowledgeable faith overflows into intimate worship. We are to live by faith. Without faith it's impossible to please God. Without faith it's even impossible to receive good gifts from God. Jesus loved it when people exhibited a strong, firm faith. By faith we are made right with God, and the righteous live by faith! Paul knew this kind of faith was essential in our lives, because the gospel he preached was that we are saved by grace through faith. Faith believes without seeing! Our walk of faith is a struggle, but part of our armor is "the shield of faith" (Ephesians 6:16), in which we use to deflect the fiery darts of the evil one! Faith is a living thing that can gush out or dribble out of us! Some of us have little faith, and others are described as having "great faith." Sometimes people destroy the faith of others, and there are those who have shipwrecked their own faith through terrible decisions. Faith can grow or faith can die. Faith without deeds is dead (or useless). Faith comes by hearing and hearing by the Word of God. The sword of the Spirit is the Word of God. The Word of God builds our faith. Jesus is the Word became flesh, the way, the truth and the life. Our faith in Jesus Christ sets us free.

I pray God will reveal Himself to you in a strong, new way and that you understand His riches, not only your eternal inheritance but also of your present access to His peace and all the spiritual blessings we have in Christ through faith. I pray God will give you a real, fresh encounter with the Gushing Springs of Jesus Christ.

## *Drink the Living Water*

"O Lord, you have searched me and you know me. You know when I sit and when I rise; you perceive my thoughts from afar. You discern my going out and my lying down; you are familiar with all my ways. Before a word is on my tongue you know it completely, O Lord." [Psalm 139:1-4]

"Now I know in part; then I shall know fully, even as I am fully known." [1 Corinthians 13:12]

"My people are destroyed from lack of knowledge." [Hosea 4:6]

"He made no distinction between us and them, for he purified their hearts by faith." [Acts 15:9]

"According to your faith will it be done to you." [Matthew 9:29]

## Deeper Reflections

— What is the connection between faith that saves and faith that motivates us to walk with God every day? (Are they the same? Are they different?)


— How deep is your Well of faith? Explain your answer.


— How would you explain your faith to someone else?


— Our woman said that the Christ would explain Himself to people. What does it mean for Christ to explain Himself to you? How has that happened in your walk with God?

— What steps are you taking to know, love, and follow God more fully?

— Are you prepared for Jesus to come back? Why or why not?

## Drenched in Prayer

*My Messiah, my Lord and Savior that I claim to know, please help me to know You as fully as You know me…to know when You sit and when You rise, to perceive Your thoughts and to discern Your comings and goings! May I continue to dip into the Well of Your Living Water and find refreshment. Give me a faith that comprehends with my mind as well as my heart. May I continue to trust You until You come again. Thank You for your grace today in my life. Amen.*

# The Declaration

*Then Jesus declared,
"I who speak to you am He."* [ John 4:26 ]

When Martha, my dear sweet mother-in-law, couldn't sleep, the next morning she'd announce to us, "I do declare, I had the big eye last night!" I have to laugh as I picture her with her pink nightcap and her big eyes! We would always laugh, and then the children would try and make their eyes pop out of their heads!

Declarations are important. When Jesus declares something, we'd better listen! He was no mere teacher, or a common man, or an ordinary prophet. Jesus teaches us in this verse is that He speaks to us, and His message is revolutionary! Today, God speaks through that still small voice of the Holy Spirit or through the Word of the God. His instructions are often present-tense directives that can involve us in

His kingdom work for that day, and His instructions need our immediate obedience. Isn't it exciting to know that Jesus speaks to His people?

*Speak to us today Lord! We're listening!*

To "declare" means, "to announce openly or formally, to show or reveal, to say emphatically." Listening, though, requires a peaceful mind and restful heart so we can pay close attention without distractions. We can listen in solitude or in the midst of the noise of the day, but stillness is a good place to start. Turn off the radio, the television, the computer, and the phone—and try not to fall asleep! You might want to take a walk and listen to the sounds of nature. Cultivating silence brings strength and an inner peace that surpasses all understanding.

This is actually the second time Jesus has declared something in His conversation with the Samaritan Woman. In verse 21, He declared for our Well Woman to believe Him. Now, in this verse we understand why. He was prepared to tell her the most astounding information the world has ever known!

As you think about this precious point in the conversation, silence your heart and listen again. Reflect on how the moment unfolded that hot day at the well. The two had bantered back and forth. Jesus invited her to take a step toward Him to trust that His intentions were good. He wasn't going to use her at all. In fact, He would be the first person in her life to really love her. She was confused about the nature of true worship. She thought it focused on a place, but He told her it should focus on a Person. Now, He told her the astounding punch line: "Then Jesus declared, 'I who speak to you am He.' "

This is Jesus' way of telling our Well Woman that He is the:

- Son of Man [John 6:27]
- Bread of Life [John 6:35]

- Light of the world [John 8:12]
- Gate for the sheep [John 10:7]
- Good shepherd [John 10:11]
- Resurrection and the life [John 11:25]
- Way and the truth and the life [John 14:6]
- Vine [John 15:1]
- Alpha and the Omega [Revelation 1:8]
- Lord God [Revelation 1:8]
- Almighty [Revelation 1:8]
- First and the Last [Revelation 1:17]
- Living One [Revelation 1:18]
- Son of God [Revelation 2:18]
- Creator [Revelation 4:11]
- Shepherd [Revelation 7:17]
- Christ [Revelation 12:10]
- Faithful and True [Revelation 19:11]
- Word of God [Revelation 19:13]
- King of kings [Revelation 19:16]
- Lord of lords [Revelation 19:16]
- Morning Star [Revelation 22:16]

What more could a girl ask for? Her knight in shining armor just rode in on a white horse! Jesus, her Messiah, had finally arrived! No more guessing. He declared His love for her by telling her who He was. And get this: Our Well Woman was the very *first* woman Jesus actually revealed Himself to as the Messiah! Not bad for a woman divorced five times!

Gushing Springs of love flooded her soul and quenched her thirst as the One and Only Living Water can do. Now that's a **WOW** moment!

## *Drink the Living Water*

Acts 13:2 "While they were worshiping the Lord and fasting, *the Holy Spirit said,* 'Set apart for me Barnabas and Saul for the work to which I have called them.'"

Isaiah 41:17-18 "The poor and needy search for water, but there is none; their tongues are parched with thirst. *But I the Lord will answer them;* I, the God of Israel, will not forsake them. I will make rivers flow on barren heights, and springs within the valleys. I will turn the desert into pools of water, and the parched ground into springs."

Revelation 1:15 "His feet were like bronze glowing in a furnace, and *his voice* was like the sound of rushing waters."

Isaiah 42:9 "See, the former things have taken place, and new things *I declare;* before they spring into being I announce them to you."

*(Italics mine.)*

## *Deeper Reflections*

— Be honest. Have you cultivated times of silence and solitude in your life in which you regularly give God opportunities to speak to you? If so, how have you benefited from these times? If not, what have you missed?

— Can you describe a time when you felt the Holy Spirit speak to you personally?


— Go back and read the list of descriptions of the Messiah. Which ones stand out to you at this point in your life? Explain your answer.


## Drenched in Prayer

*My Messiah, I declare my love for You today. I want to know You as personally and as intimately as the Samaritan Woman at the Well that day. As I cultivate time and silence into my day, speak to my own heart as You did hers. I have faith that Your perfect love has driven out all fears that keep me from hearing You. As I open Your Word and seek You today, I know I'll find You. I love You. Amen.*

# The Advance and the Testimony

# Just Listen

*Just then His disciples returned and were surprised to find Him talking with a woman. But no one asked, "What do you want?" or "Why are you talking with her?"* [John 4:27]

alk about bad timing and dead silence! Doesn't it always work that way? Right when something really good is happening, something else messes it up. I used to believe it was just "bad luck," but now I know it could be caused by several other things, such as spiritual warfare, living in a fallen world, God's pruning or discipline, or just plain old bad choices! God uses every situation, no matter what the cause, to teach us and mold us. In Jesus' encounter with the Samaritan Woman, the conversation was at the pivotal point. At that precise time, a bunch of guys (Wouldn't you know it?!) barged in on that intimate moment. Watch carefully to see the response.

You just gotta love these guys! They come back from town with sack lunches (probably super-sized!) and find Jesus talking to a not only a woman, but to a *Samaritan* Woman who had a questionable reputation. "Man," they may have thought, "we can't leave that guy alone for a minute!" We have to hand it to them. At least they were sensitive enough to know that this wasn't the time to be asking questions! (I can remember many times in my life when I've been surprised at something or someone, and the first thing I did was blurt out what I was thinking. Then "foot-in-mouth syndrome" sets in, and then...well, you know the story! Sometimes your spiritual gift can be your worst enemy if you aren't careful! James 1:19 says, "My dear brothers, take note of this: Everyone should be quick to listen, slow to speak...")

One of the hardest disciplines I've had to cultivate in my Christian life is listening to God. As the leader of the Women of the Well Ministry, one of the most important things I can do is listen to the Lord, because it truly is His ministry, and I need to follow His leading every day. One day while I was eating lunch at the kitchen table, I heard the Lord speak audibly to me: "I have something to say to you." In mid-bite, I dropped my turkey and Swiss with mayo smack dab in the middle of my plate and literally hit my knees in reverence—or holy fear! He continued in a still small voice this time: "If you listen, I will send you." I guess you could say it was one of those "power lunches"!

Ever since that day, I've always checked myself to see who I am listening to. The enemy wants to jam our communication with Christ by over-stimulating our minds by enticing us to play our TV's, VCR's DVD's, CD's, MVP's, PC's—and any other ABBR's you can think of! We make listening to God so hard, and yet He really wants to speak to us. During the transfiguration of Jesus, a cloud appeared and enveloped Peter, James, John and Jesus on the mountain (see Mark 9:7), then a voice came from the cloud and said, "This is my Son, whom I love. Listen to Him!" There you have it ladies, straight from the Master: Listen to Him!

God speaks to us in many ways: through wise friends or teachers, our spirits, our circumstances, nature, and through His Word. Some messages we hear each day are helpful and positive, but others are confusing and contradictory to what the Word says. Let me urge you to always use God's Word as your sword in combat and your filter for voices that bring confusion, doubt, fear, or false guilt. God's Word is always our plumb line of truth.

Here's a fun little side Bible Study for you that only takes a minute: Look up in the Book of Revelation these passages: 2:7, 2:11, 2:17, 2:29, 3:6, 3:13 and 3:22. Do you see it? The same message was given for us seven different times! (Seven in the bible represents wholeness.) I hope it speaks to your spirit as you find time this week to hear with your spiritual ears.

I love each of you, and I'm praying for you.

## Drink the Living Water

"This day I call heaven and earth as witnesses against you that I have set before you life and death, blessings and curses. Now choose life, so that you and your children may live and that you may love the Lord your God, listen to his voice, and hold fast to him. For the Lord is your life, and he will give you many years in the land he swore to give to your fathers, Abraham, Isaac and Jacob." [Deuteronomy 30:19-20]

"The Lord called Samuel a third time, and Samuel got up and went to Eli and said, 'Here I am; you called me.' The Eli realized that the Lord was calling the boy. So Eli told Samuel, 'Go and lie down, and if he calls you, say, "Speak, Lord, for your servant is listening." ' So Samuel went and lay down in his place. The Lord came and stood there, calling as at the other times, 'Samuel! Samuel!' Then Samuel said, 'Speak, for your servant is listening.'" [1 Samuel 3:8-10]

"As Jesus and his disciples were on their way, he came to a village where a woman named Martha opened her home to him. She had a sister called Mary, who sat at the Lord's feet listening to what he said." [Luke 10:38-39]

## *Deeper Reflections*

— How do you normally react to interruptions and difficulties? What could you do differently?

— What are some ways to tell if an impression is from God or not?

— What do you hear God saying to you these days?

— What do you hear God saying to our society, our government, and our world?

## Drenched in Prayer

*Today, sit still and be where you are, (not thinking of all the things you should be doing.). Breathe out all unforgiveness, bitterness, and anger. Lay all burdens and worries on the altar. Then just sit and listen. Close your eyes now, and let God speak to you. He may remind you of a passage of Scripture, or He may prompt you to take action to care for someone in need. Continue to do this each day for longer periods until you have cultivated the discipline of listening. Don't be discouraged if you don't hear anything at first. Seek first His Kingdom and His righteousness, and all these things will be given to you as well. (Matthew 6:33)*

# *Advance!*

*Leaving her water jar, the woman went back to the town and said to the people, "Come and see a man who told me everything I ever did."* [ John 4:28 ]

This is the beginning of the last scene in our drama, and also one of those "Aha!" moments! Have you ever noticed that the Woman at the Well forgot her reason for coming to the well in the first place—leaving her water jar behind? This shamed, withdrawn woman had come at the hottest hour of the day when no others came to draw water in order to escape ridicule, embarrassment, and the haughty stares of others, but she was now speaking to an entire town. Amazing Grace!

How did she get from point A to point Z, from needing and hiding to overflowing and sharing? Simple enough. One little trip to the well, and one encounter with a Man who wouldn't turn her away or use and abuse her. One large gulp of the true drink of Living Water. One big step forward without looking back.

Her meeting with Jesus was a supernatural encounter. If she had been confronted by harsh accusation or silent condemnation, she would have run away. But Jesus met her with love and compassion. His goal was not to punish her but to redeem her. His gift of grace and mercy brings eternal life and transforms even the hardest of hearts.

Though we are often reminded in the Scriptures to "look back at the cross of Christ," we need to make sure we look back at the forgiveness Jesus gives us and not focus only on our sins that needed to be forgiven. One brings freedom; the other brings the bondage of fear and doubt again.

Our Well Woman wasn't looking back. She was going forward in grace, in truth, and with a new confidence. Her old reputation was overcome, and she became a new creation! Can you imagine the freedom she felt? She now knew she had been cleansed from her past. Her daily, dull, routine, lonely trip to the well had turned into an adventure that changed her life forever! Oh, how I wish I could have been there that day!

But yes, we can be there ourselves! We can meet Jesus at the Well of Living Water everyday. No exceptions. We can take our bottles, cups, or buckets full of guilt, confusion, humiliation, worry, or inadequacy and leave them there with Him—just like the Samaritan Woman did. After encountering our loving Messiah, we can *walk away in faith*, knowing He already knows the whole story about us, and He loves us still. We can be filled with His Spirit so we too can pour His love into others. We need to *go* in faith, *ask* through prayer, and *receive* His best!

As we experience God's love and strength, we become true Women of the Well. Our identity changes, and the accusations of others are replaced with the acceptance of Almighty God. Here is what the

Word of God says of our identity, straight from the Well, to count on whenever we choose to leave our own water pots behind:

- I am forgiven all my sins and washed in the blood. [Ephesians 1:7]
- I am a new creature. [2 Corinthians 5:17]
- I am the temple of the Holy Spirit. [1 Corinthians 6:19]
- I am delivered from the power of darkness. [Colossians 1:13]
- I am strong in the Lord. [Ephesians 6:10]
- I am holy and without blame before Him. [Ephesians 1:4]
- I am accepted in Christ. [Ephesians 1:6]
- I am qualified to share in His inheritance. [Colossians 1:12]
- I am victorious. [Revelation 21:7]
- I am dead to sin. [Romans 6:2, 11]
- I am loved with an everlasting love. [Jeremiah 31:3]
- I am set free! [John 8:31-33]
- I am raised up with Christ and seated in the heavenly places. [Colossians 2:12]
- I am more than a conqueror! [Romans 8:37]
- I am beloved of God. [1 Thessalonians 1:4]
- I am born of God and the evil one does not touch me. [1 John 5:18]
- I am a joint heir with Christ. [Romans 8:17]
- I am reconciled to God. [2 Corinthians 5:18]
- I am overtaken with blessings! [Deuteronomy 28:2]
- I am sealed with the promise of the Holy Spirit. [Ephesians 1:13]
- I am complete in Christ. [Colossians 2:10]
- I am free from condemnation. [Romans 8:1]
- I am firmly rooted, built up, strengthened in the faith, and overflowing with thankfulness. [Colossians 2:7]
- I am being changed into His image. [Philippians 1:6]

- I have all my needs met by God according to His glorious riches in Christ Jesus. [Philippians 4:19]
- I have the mind of Christ. [1 Corinthians 2:16]
- I have everlasting life. [John 6:47]
- I have abundant life. [John 10:10]
- I have the peace of God which passes understanding. [Philippians 4:7]
- I have access to the Father by one Spirit. [Ephesians 2:18]
- I can do all things through Jesus Christ. [Philippians 4:13]
- I shall do even greater works than Christ Jesus. [John 14:12]
- I possess the Greater One in me because greater is He in me than he who is in the world. [1 John 4:4]
- I know God's voice. [John 10:14]
- Christ is in me the hope of glory! [Colossians 1:27]

Even though her time with Jesus was interrupted by the guys coming back from lunch, our Samaritan Woman walked away forgiven, highly favored, fulfilled, free, and going forward, not looking back! Instantly, the love of God overflowed from her and she told everybody she knew about Jesus. She didn't wait to take a spiritual gifts test, she didn't attend seminary, she didn't consult her pastor or anyone else to look for approval or confirmation, no one laid hands on her, and by golly, it doesn't even say she prayed before she went to town! And she went into the town filled with the same people she had been afraid of just minutes before! What happened to her fear of their accusations and condemnation? These were people she had feared, slept with, been married to, divorced from, mistreated and despised by, and only God knows what else. But she went there, overflowing with the truth and love and grace of our Lord Jesus Christ, standing firm on her belief and her newfound security, *advancing* the Kingdom of God! Her response makes me think about my own grasp of God's grace. Does it make you think about yours, too?

Our Well Woman (and *well* she was now) launched a full-scale evangelism campaign all by her little self! Who says one person can't make a difference? She simply gave out what she had taken in.

Her attitude and behavior were changed because she met and trusted Jesus Christ. He didn't walk up to her and give her a command to take the gospel to her neighbors. First, He initiated a conversation. Gradually, He won her trust. She believed He was the Messiah, who could cleanse her from her sins, and then, she was so overcome with joy, she delighted in telling everyone who would listen about Him! That overflow can't happen when we are clogged with guilt and shame. First, we have to encounter Jesus and have Him cleanse us. Then the Holy Spirit can flow through us. The order is absolutely essential. It never varies. We simply cannot and will not overflow until and unless the clogs of bitterness and selfishness are cleaned out from our hearts. When that happens, watch out! The Well of God's love and grace is deep, and it gushes out from us!

Our woman met Jesus. Then she was known and loved. She needed no more masks, and she no longer needed to pretend. She was happy and had peace about it! That about says it all, ladies, let's quit retreating and let's *advance!*

## Drink the Living Water

"Now to each one the manifestation of the Spirit is given for the common good." [1 Corinthians 12:7]

"You, my brothers, were called to be free. But do not use your freedom to indulge the sinful nature, rather, serve one another in love. The entire law is summed up in a single command: 'Love your neighbor as yourself.' If you keep on biting and devouring each other, watch out or you will be destroyed by each other." [Galatians 5:13-15]

"It is for freedom that Christ has set us free. Stand firm, then, and do not let yourselves be burdened again by a yoke of slavery." [Galatians 5:1]

"As soon as they had brought them out, one of them said, 'Flee for your lives! *Don't look back,* and don't stop anywhere in the plain! Flee to the mountains or you will be swept away!'" [Genesis 19:17]
*(Italics mine.)*

## *Deeper Reflections*
— What are some ways you can tell that the Samaritan Woman has been transformed?

— Are you prepared to leave your water bucket behind today? If so, what was in it? What is it replaced with now?

— What does the overflow of joy look like in your life? Who do you want to tell about what God has done for you? How will you tell them? If you're not willing to tell anyone, what's hindering you?

## Drenched in Prayer

*Jesus, meet me today. Take the water bottle of things I think I want and in exchange, fill me with that same Living Water You offered the Samaritan Woman many years ago. I have faith that You won't turn me away, judge me, or punish me, but that You will be compassionate and loving in an unconditional way. Help me to receive by faith all that You have for me today and to take it to others in a loving way that glorifies You. Amen.*

# *The Hope*

*"Could this be the Christ?"* [ John 4:29 ]

*H*ope. Can you hear it in this question?

"Could this be the Christ?"

On the rollaway bed at the hospital, I was in recovery from my operation, opening my eyes and trying to focus. As the blur cleared, I saw my husband standing near me like I had never seen him before. His eyes welled up with tears. "What is it?" I asked as I awoke from the anesthesia.

He told me with a powerful blend of joy and relief, "It wasn't there, the tumor was gone. I've witnessed a miracle today!"

That day, hope came through and faith was built. I had held tight to Jesus. I also received a new level of understanding of what Jesus, the suffering Servant, experienced for us on Calvary—though I doubt our human minds can ever comprehend such love mixed with such intolerable suffering. Jesus knew exactly what He would have to endure, but "for the joy set before Him, He endured the cross" for you and me. His obedience to the Father's will, brought Him through the darkest moment in all of history in order to give us a hope that never dies.

Then my husband whispered softly, "Thank you, Jesus." Others may have doubted, but Jesus glorified Himself through the miracle of healing. The doctors just couldn't understand it. They could give no explanation for the report. But I knew. Even though I had a six-inch incision on my lower abdomen, the tumor was gone just as I had suspected it was.

"Could this be the Christ?" some asked me through questioning eyes.

"Yes, it could be, and yes, it was," I answered.

The H in Hope stands for *holding* tight to Jesus.

The O stands for *obedience* to the Word of God.

The P in Hope stands for *prayer* that never ceases.

The E in Hope stands for *enduring* until the end.

I'm filled with hope today as I reflect on the story of our Woman at the Well, aren't you? Patient, hope-filled endurance will build our faith and will help us see God more clearly. Our prayers are an expression of our hope. And He answers our prayers according to His gracious promises to give wisdom, strength, and grace in times of trouble.

In 1 Corinthians 13:13, Paul says, "And now these three remain; faith, hope and love." Hope is inextricably related to our faith and God's love. In fact, hope is sandwiched between faith and love.

In Hebrews 11:1, the writer says, "Faith is being sure of what we hope for." And in 1 Corinthians 13:7, Paul again says, "Love always hopes." Hope, then, has to be rooted in faith to produce change, and the fuel for our hope is the abounding, astounding love of God.

Without Christ's forgiveness, we have no hope for redemption from our pasts, deliverance from our present, or salvation for our futures. We can try to fill that longing in our souls with alcohol, material possessions, status, food, sex, friends, pornography, or whatever flirts with our fancy, but nothing brings hope like Jesus does. He was obedient to the point of death on the cross because of His love for us, and His sacrifice forgave us of all our sins. His resurrection from the dead and ascension into heaven assure us of our ultimate hope of eternal life with Him.

Our Woman at the Well found hope on that day through Jesus Christ, the Messiah. Her spontaneous and glad response shows that she had no doubt what she had found. Salvation was hers for the taking—and she took it. She went through the stages of restoration, first by surrendering herself, then being honest about her past, accepting Jesus' forgiveness and His healing of her hurts, entering into an intimate relationship with Jesus, accepting the Living Water, and finally worshipping God. Now in scene four of our story, we find her being released into ministry. Her hope has found its destiny, and her life has new purpose. God's plan to reach the whole world with His love is being orchestrated through the life of a woman who was broken and lost only moments before. She is now the aroma of Christ to everyone she meets. Beautiful are the feet of those who bring the good news!

# *Drink the Living Water*

"May the God of hope fill you with all joy and peace as you trust in Him, so that you may overflow with hope by the power of the Holy Spirit." [Romans 15: 13]

"We always thank God, the Father of our Lord Jesus Christ, when we pray for you, because we have heard of your faith in Christ Jesus and of the love you have for all the saints—the faith and love that spring from the hope that is stored up for you in heaven and that you have already heard about in the word of truth, the gospel that has come to you." [Colossians 1:3-5]

"But now he has reconciled you by Christ's physical body through death to present you holy in his sight, without blemish and free from accusation – if you continue in your faith, established and firm, not moved from the hope held out in the gospel." [Colossians 1:22-23]

"To them God has chosen to make known among the Gentiles the glorious riches of this mystery, which is Christ in you, the hope of glory." [Colossians 1:27]

"We continually remember before our God and Father your work produced by faith, your labor prompted by love, and your endurance inspired by hope in our Lord Jesus Christ." [1 Thessalonians 1:3]

"Why are you downcast, O my soul? Why so disturbed within me? Put your hope in God for I will yet praise him, my Savior and My God." [Psalm 42:5]

## *Deeper Reflections*

— Hope comes from hearing, and hearing from the Word of God. Today, read each of the Scripture references, and answer these questions:

• How does the passage describe the source of our hope?

• How does the passage describe our response to this hope?

## *Drenched in Prayer*

*Dear Father, thank You for sending the Christ child for me. His birth was a miracle in itself! Help me to hold tight to Jesus in these tough times and to be obedient to Your Word. Help me to build a faith that endures and a prayer life that never quits. When it seems all hope is lost, help me to remember that You can do absolutely anything. I want to always remember this Woman at the Well and what one encounter with Jesus Christ did for her. Allow me to be an instrument of Your peace and the hope I find in You. Amen.*

# The Testimony

*Many of the Samaritans from that town believed in Him because of the woman's testimony.* [John 4:39]

Have you ever noticed that the word *testimony* includes two t's. The first t begins a word within the word: *test*. Whether we like it or not, we can't have a testimony unless we have first been tested.

The second t could stand for *teacher*, because now the tables are turned and our Samaritan Woman teaches her neighbors about the Messiah. But the second t could also stand for *trust*. Faith, hope, and confidence are the hidden strengths of anyone's testimony. We can't give a powerful testimony as the Woman from the Well did without trusting that we have seen, been with, experienced, believed, and accepted the grace and power of Jesus Christ.

When we step out of our comfort zones to share our testimony about God's faithfulness, someone will always be affected by it—in this case it was "many" people.

God may have tested you in one or more areas of your life. His purpose in testing us is to deepen and purify our trust in Him. I can think of several leaps of faith in my own life that have developed a deeper trust in God, and also some amazing testimonies of His faithfulness! Each time we are tested, we not only are faced with a leap of faith, but we also leave something behind—we pick up our cross and lay down something of our own. This is part of denying ourselves, surrendering to Him, and following Him. I often urge my children to leave behind something (namely television) in order to prepare for a test that they may have in school the next day. Similarly, when we have tests, we often not only give up something, but also learn something new.

What did the Samaritan Woman leave behind? She left her sinful life, her condemnation, her emptiness, her loneliness, her worldly cares, and her confusion. She left behind her water pots of shame and guilt! Ladies, she got over it! She traded in her tension and chaos for trust and peace! Jesus truly is our bridge over troubled waters! She got over the past rejections. She witnessed joyfully because Jesus had set her free from her past. Nobody had to force her to tell people about Him. She was thrilled to tell them! He was her Messiah after all! Alleluia!

What did she testify about? That's not the right question. It's not "what," but rather "who." Our God, Jesus, Lord, Savior, Almighty, Abba, Father, Prince of Peace and Truth are just a few of the names of the wonderful "Who" we testify about. In John 14:6 Jesus proclaims, "I am the way, and the truth and the life." It's our pleasure and privilege to proclaim the same message.

Our testimony of faith in Christ is almost always the result of someone else sharing his or her testimony with us. We can't trust God until we have heard about Him. In Romans 10:14-15, Paul tells us, "How, then, can they call on the one they have not believed in? And how can they believe in the one of whom they have not heard? And how can they hear without someone preaching to them? And how can they preach unless they are sent? As it is written, 'How beautiful are the feet of those who bring good news!' "

That day in Samaria, it was the beautiful feet of Jesus who brought the Good News in person to the Woman at the Well. But by the end of the day, the Samaritan Woman's testimony about Jesus was carried to the people of her town by her own beautiful feet. She was now the one Gushing Springs of Living Water out to all! This is an amazing fact. The one who had been so rejected, ashamed, and alone became the spokesperson for God's grace. And she brought it to both men and women alike. In fact, the first person we see doing evangelism was a woman! In Liz Curtis Higg's book, *Bad Girls of the Bible*, she says, "The Samaritan woman taught not with books but with her life. Her faith couldn't be contained. It flowed through every crack and crevice of her being." In other words, she didn't ask people to give their lives to God, but rather, her new and exciting life from God was flowing all over the neighborhood! And the results were nothing short of astonishing!

Truth travels by way of testimony. Testimony travels by way of beautiful feet. Share your testimony and tell about the truth of Jesus Christ, and "Many will believe!" Whether you are a witness to Jesus' truth in your home, your pulpit, your work, your neighborhood, or among the poor or abused, remember that our lives speak volumes.

Go ahead, I dare you! Get over it, and go for it!

---

4   Liz Curtiz Higgs, *Bad Girls of the Bible*, Waterbrook Press, Colorado Springs, CO, 1999, pg. 101

## Drink the Living Water

"All authority in heaven and on earth has been given to me. Therefore go and make disciples of all nations, baptizing them in the name of the Father and of the Son and of the Holy Spirit, and teaching them to obey everything I have commanded you. And surely I am with you always." [Matthew 28:18-20]

"All this is from God, who reconciled us to himself through Christ and gave us the ministry of reconciliation: that God was reconciling the world to himself in Christ, not counting men's sins against them. And he has committed to us the message of reconciliation. We are therefore Christ's ambassadors, as though God were making his appeal through us." [2 Corinthians 5:18-20]

"And this gospel of the kingdom will be preached in the whole world as a testimony to all nations, and then the end will come." [Matthew 24:14]

"They overcame him by the blood of the Lamb and by the word of their testimony;" [Revelation 12:11]

"But in your hearts set apart Christ as Lord. Always be prepared to give an answer to everyone who asks you to give the reason for the hope that you have. But do this with gentleness and respect, keeping a clear conscience, so that those who speak maliciously against your good behavior in Christ may be ashamed of their slander." [1 Peter 3, 15, 16]

"Be wise in the way you act toward outsiders; make the most of every opportunity. Let your conversation be always full of grace, seasoned with salt, so that you may know how to answer everyone." [Colossians 4:5, 6]

## Deeper Reflections

— Imagine the expression on the woman's face as she left Jesus, and imagine her running back to town without her water pot and stopping every person on the street to tell them about her meeting with Jesus. Describe what you think may have been going on in her heart at this moment to give her such unrestrained joy.

— When have you experienced this kind of unrestrained joy in your relationship with Jesus?

— Sharing the Good News about Christ is the one thing we won't be able to do in heaven. Who would you like to tell about Jesus love?

— What are some ways Jesus has changed your life?

— Write out your testimony, including:
  * Describe what your life was like before you trusted Him.
  * What happened to surface your need for a Savior?
  * Describe the specifics of the event when you trusted Christ to save you.
  * Describe one specific change that God has made in your life since then.

# Drenched in Prayer

*Lord, I'm a vessel filled with the Living Water of your Truth. Your Spirit lives inside me. Take me to a place today where I can sing Your praises and toot Your horn! I desire to pour out to others this Gushing Spring that brings rest, peace, joy and love! How could I ever keep such a gift to myself? Help me to not be greedy with my time, but to pour out Your love and strength to all I come in contact with! Refresh me and restore me to the point that I too am bubbling over like the Woman at the Well. Thank You for never giving up on me, Lord, and including me Your plan to save a lost and hurting world. Give me wisdom to now to write out my own testimony. I love You Lord. Amen.*

# Women in Ministry

*So when the Samaritans came to Him, they urged Him to stay with them, and He stayed two days. And because of His words many more became believers. They said to the woman, "We no longer believe just because of what you said; now we have heard for ourselves, and we know that this man really is the Savior of the world."* [ John 4:40–42 ]

This scene is amazing to me. The people in our Well Woman's neighborhood are now coming to Jesus! These are the same men and women who once degraded her, treating her as an outcast, labeling her "untouchable, unapproachable and unlovable." But now they're believing her testimony and trusting her account of her meeting with Jesus! First they heard her testimony, and because of the power of her message, they believed her in spite of their previous judgments of her. The statement "just because of what you said" in verse 42 tells me they weren't being critical of her—they were actually agreeing with her because their time with Jesus corroborated her testimony of His grace and truth.

After the people heard the woman tell them about Jesus, they came to Jesus to hear for themselves and become believers—and then get this: They held a two-day revival with Him! (This is one revival I want to see a playback of in heaven!) Did you realize that this story represents the first instance of cross-cultural evangelism in the New Testament? The Samaritans and the Jews were traditional enemies, but God bridged that gap. How awesome is that?

This event was also Jesus' first unqualified and unopposed success in ministry recorded in John's gospel. His own people in Galilee and Judea always wanted Him to "qualify" Himself with miracles and healing because they didn't believe Jesus was who He claimed to be. Their hearts were hardened. But the Samaritan Woman's neighbors believed. Don't you just love this story?

In the first century in Palestine, women were second class citizens, but Jesus used *a woman* to convert a whole town. As we read the gospel accounts, we find that women are a vital part of Jesus' ministry. In Julie R. Wilson's book, *Restoring your Spiritual Heritage,*[5] she writes, "Women in ministry have long been a thorn in the Church's side. In light of the wealth of scriptural precedent for women in ministry which the Bible affords, I am not sure why. In both the Old and New Testaments, women supplied nearly every role within the Church. Deborah served as judge; Bathsheba as queen mother; Ester as intercessor; Anna and

---

5    Julie R. Wilson, *Restoring Your Spiritual Heritage,* Faith Walk Publishing, 2004, pg. 134

Mary of Bethany as prophets; Mary Magdalene as evangelist; Priscilla as teacher; and Phoebe as apostle or deaconess, just to name a few. Women supported Jesus' ministry through their finances, hospitality, prayers, prophetic acts and worship—and He didn't seem to have a problem with any of it, even when his disciples did (Mt. 26:6-13). In fact, Jesus regularly elevated women's status by entrusting them with privileged information and relationship with him despite social and religious opposition." I wholeheartedly agree. (And did you catch the part about Deborah as judge? I really like that part!)

This role of women is an important issue that must be settled in the church and in the hearts of God's people. God is no respecter of persons, and He doesn't play favorites. This story of the Woman at the Well is an excellent example of His perspective about the role of women. We could cite many stories in the Bible of women God used in ministry, and we could discuss a certain verse Paul wrote that has been taken out of context by far to many men and women. But when you take the whole counsel of God into consideration, and we see the gifted ministries of such women today as Beth Moore, Joyce Meyer, Jennifer Rothschild, and Paula White, there can be no argument that God desires women to use the gifts He has given them for His glory. Amen! So let's just give our Samaritan Woman a big round of applause for a job well done in her love and obedience to Christ—and quit playing the games about the role of women!

## Drink the Living Water

"However, I consider my life worth nothing to me, if only I may finish the race and complete the task the Lord Jesus has given me—the task of testifying to the gospel of God's grace." [Acts 20:24]

"But the Lord said to Samuel, 'Do not consider his appearance or his height, for I have rejected him. The Lord does not look at the things man looks at. Man looks at the outward appearance, but the Lord looks at the heart.'" [1 Samuel 16:7]

"For God does not show favoritism." [Romans 2:11]

## *Deeper Reflections*

— Is it significant to you that God used a woman as His first example of a person reaching a town with the Good News about Christ? Explain your answer.

— What is your understanding of women in ministry in the church?

— Why do you suppose Satan prefers that women do not exercise our gifts?

# Drenched in Prayer

*Oh Lord, please give me wisdom, peace, and a clear understand-
ing to what Your will is for my life. Let there be no questions
in my mind, so that the enemy may not undermine Your plans.
Help me to stand firm in Your purpose for me and to be as effective as the Samaritan Woman was. May my life be a clear
reflection and overflow of the extravagant love You have for me.
It's time for me to stop being the bridesmaid, and be the Bride
You called me to be! Help me to not only be all You meant me
to be, to have all You meant me to have, but also to love all You
meant me to love. All praise and glory to the beautiful, sweet,
name of Jesus. Amen.*

# The Harvest and the Workers

# Springboarding Truths

*Meanwhile His disciples urged him, "Rabbi, eat something." But He said to them, "I have food to eat you know nothing about." Then His disciples said to each other, "Could someone have brought Him food?"*

[ John 4:31–33 ]

I'll have to be honest, if I'm urged to eat "something," my first choice is most definitely chocolate! Yes, I'm a die-hard chocoholic and so is my daughter, Cristahl! The apple (chocolate covered of course) doesn't fall far from the tree. (And in case you missed it, that's her on the cover!) We just love our chocolate. In this interaction with the disciples, Jesus used food as a springboard to show us a great example of God-honoring priorities.

Throughout Jesus' ministry, His disciples were often preoccupied with food. I can relate. (Is that why I'm always on a diet?) But Jesus was always pointing them back to God to seek His Kingdom first. God knew their needs, and He promised to provide every single time. Jesus' life was the supreme example of someone who is completely dedicated to the purposes and priorities of Almighty God. Jesus continued to tantalize them with parables, mysteries, stories and secrets that whet their appetites to teach them about spiritual thirst. You would have thought by now these guys would have been enlightened to His ways! But on the other hand, have you ever noticed that Jesus hardly ever gave anyone in our story a straight answer? And here again, He uses an earthly metaphor to teach a spiritual truth, the same thing He did with our Samaritan Woman, who was now on the way to the town they had just returned from! And who says women aren't quick to understand? By golly, I bet she may have even been a blonde!

The disciples brought lunch to Jesus, but He told them He had food they didn't know anything about. Can't you see these men looking around Him for the fish sticks, loaves, rice, a fire, several great gourmet chefs, a burning bush, or anything else Jesus had stashed? Can't you just imagine what was going through their minds? "Food, what food? I don't see any lamb burgers and fries!" "Hey, didn't He just send us into town for food?"

I know my husband—if he had been walking all day in the hot sun to find a grocery store, and when he got home I told him I had food he knew nothing about…well, let's just say he wouldn't be too thrilled with the idea! He has a hard enough time finding the jelly in the refrigerator, much less hunting items on a list at the grocery store! (I apologize to any men reading this, including my husband.) But I love my man just the same!

For the second time in our story, Jesus used physical needs of thirst (with the woman) and hunger (with the disciples) to teach spiritual lessons.

Years ago I prepared lunch for a group of men. It was a Monday morning, and we were in the middle of building our home. Even though I had heard God speak to me in the early morning hours—like He often does—saying, *"Tuesday* is the day you should take lunch to your builders," I told the foreman in charge, "My husband and I would like to bring lunch for all of you on *Thursday."*

I'd seen the weather report. The forecast for Tuesday was rain and cool weather, but Thursday was to be sunny and dry. Besides, I couldn't possibly get everything together in one day to feed ten to twelve men. When God told Isaiah to go, he responded, "Here am I, Lord. Send me!" But I said, "Here I am, Lord. Send me on Thursday!"

As I approached the foreman, I felt uneasy. I knew in my heart that God wanted it done on Tuesday. These men had been working since November on our home in snowstorms, ice storms, and many days in temperatures well below freezing. As I spoke to the foreman, I could see a worried look in his eyes. His response to me explained his expression. He told me, "But ma'am, tomorrow is our last day here."

I thought to myself, "Okay, Tuesday it is, God!" I replied to the foreman, "That's fine, we'll do it tomorrow. Please let your guys know not to bring lunch."

Now I was in a bind. I had less than twenty-four hours to pull this thing off. But when God leads, God provides. Everything came together beautifully. That night, my husband and I loaded a table into the truck with nine folding chairs. Some would have to eat standing up or sitting on buckets.

The next morning we prayed together asking God to help us show love and gratitude to these men who seemed very downcast and burdened. I set up the table and the chairs. One of the workers was so excited about the lunch he actually swept out the room where we were to eat. By lunchtime, every inch of table space was covered with food. Psalm 23 came to mind: "You prepare a table before me." We were ready for the men to come.

My husband pulled down the driveway right on time. The hungry men followed him, and we all sat down. To my surprise, some of the men had been pulled off the job that morning, and there were only five men, my husband and I. At first I was disappointed. I silently complained, "All this delicious food and no one even shows up!" But then I thought," What a nice cozy number for conversation!" Two empty chairs were left.

Minutes later, a giant semi truck drove down the driveway. A man was delivering one tiny tube of caulking! I invited this Lone Ranger to lunch. After all, we still had space and plenty of goodies. He gladly accepted. This truck driver intrigued me. During the whole meal, he never spoke a word, but he listened intently. (He stayed the whole hour-and-a-half as we ate and talked about how God had transformed our lives and our marriage through His love. Then the man got up, thanked us and left. I'm convinced God wanted me to prepare that lunch specifically for that man, or perhaps he was an angel. Someday I hope to find out.) I realized that after he sat down, we only had one empty chair. Jesus sat there.

The conversation just flowed like water from a well (Sorry, I couldn't help myself!), even though we really didn't know these men. God led as we told our stories of how He had delivered, healed, redeemed, and rescued us so many times. They told their stories and shared their needs. We encouraged them and tried to offer help in different ways. We welcomed them as the first guests in our brand new home, and we thanked them for all their hard work. They acted as if no one had ever thanked them before—nor fed them! The best part was knowing Jesus was there, too. We may never know exactly what happened in their hearts that day. But we do know God sent us, and we went. Similar to Jesus, we used food as a springboard to highlight some spiritual truths.

That was a rich, rewarding experience, but I almost missed it because I didn't want to do exactly what God instructed me to do. We need to respond in faith when we say, "Here I am, Lord. Send me!" When God sends us, we may or may not understand the entirety of our mission. That's the situation when the disciples returned from town with lunch that day! *Our job is to be obedient, and leave the results up to God.*

## Drink the Living Water

"In the morning, O Lord, you hear my voice; in the morning I lay my requests before you and wait in expectation." [Psalm 5:3]

"Then Jesus said to his disciples: 'Therefore I tell you, do not worry about your life, what you will eat; or about your body, what you will wear. Life is more than food, and the body more than clothes. Consider the ravens: They do not sow or reap, they have no storeroom or barn; yet God feeds them. And how much more valuable you are than birds! Who of you by worrying can add a single hour to his life? Since you cannot do this very little thing, why do you worry about the rest?'" [Luke 12:22-26]

"Then Jesus declared, 'I am the bread of life. He who comes to me will never go hungry, and he who believes in me will never be thirsty. But as I told you, you have seen me and still you do not believe. All that the Father gives me will come to me, and whoever comes to me I will never drive away. For I have come down from heaven not to do my will but to do the will of him who sent me. And this is the will of him who sent me, that I shall lose none of all that he has given me, but raise them up at the last day. For my Father's will is that everyone who looks to the Son and believes in him shall have eternal life, and I will raise him up at the last day.'" [John 6:35-48]

"Do not forget to entertain strangers, for by so doing some people have entertained angels without knowing it." [Hebrews 13:2]

## *Deeper Reflections*
— What do you imagine the disciples were thinking when Jesus told them He had food they didn't know about?


— Why do you think Jesus often used food and drink to communicate spiritual truths? Can you think of any other places in the Bible that Jesus uses physical things to springboard to spiritual truths?

— What are some ways you have used hospitality to share the love of God with others?

— Be honest, if you heard God ask you to do something totally out of your comfort zone, would you do it? Why or why not? Give examples.

## Drenched in Prayer

*Jesus, You are my Bread of Life, my Living Water and I cannot live without You. I praise You today for teaching me about courage, about provision, and about Your kindness. Your grace is truly amazing in all circumstances, and Your love truly drives out fear. There's a lot more food You have for me that I don't know anything about, Lord. Please show me through revelations, dreams, impressions, and even visions those things You died to give me, and protect me from all confusion and doubt along the way. Lord, send me! I love You! Amen.*

# Our Slice of Life

*"My food," said Jesus, "is to do the will of Him who sent me and to finish His work."*

[ John 4:34 ]

*J*esus' teachings sometimes sound really strange. This is one of those. Is He talking about food, is He talking about wills, or is He talking about work? He sure can say a mouthful in a Kansas City second!

Speaking of mouthfuls, I just got back from a speaking engagement in good old Alabama! That Southern hospitality was over the top! Those ladies sure know how to make a girl feel welcome! It was comparable to something so delicious you just want to devour it—like a big piece of triple chocolate mousse cake with double fudge whipped cream icing, heated, with a huge scoop of the best vanilla ice cream around! Jesus saw His role as delicious, and that role, of course, was to reach *us*. This perspective also explains why He had such a passion for doing the will of His Father. He just ate off one little bite at a time until the big job was finished.

Many of us have a hard time finishing things. Oh, we start one project, and then start something else, and then maybe even start something else, till we have so much going on, that hey, we forget what it was we originally set out to do. We end up finishing absolutely nothing. Or we might start thinking about a new idea, put it down "for a rest" and intend to pick it back up later, but we always seem to find something else more interesting, so we don't come back to it. Am I speaking to the choir here, or what?!

Is it my imagination, or is it true that many of us get so busy that we find it hard to do any *one* thing with godly excellence these days? This is why I love this passage in John's gospel. Every single verse is packed with power for every one of us.

Speaking personally, I probably need to try to do less, but do it with more excellence. But I think, "If I tried just a little harder I could do it all!" That propels me to commit myself to do more and more, but I accomplish less and less. Well, I obviously have a problem!

So what's the solution? It's solitude. God has been speaking to us since He breathed creation into being, and He hasn't stopped speaking. Jesus is called "The Word" because it is His nature to communicate with us. Through the Scriptures and by impressions of the Holy Spirit, God will talk to us if we are willing to stop at the Well and have a little cake with Him. We need to feed ourselves spiritually as well as physically. Our spiritual strength comes not only from what we take in, though, but also by what we pour out. As our hearts become one with Christ, we will care about the things He cares about, and we will take action to obey Him just as He obeyed the Father. When we give ourselves over to God's will, we will fulfill the destiny He has planned for us!

So eat a bite with Jesus, then eat some more, focusing on God's will for your life, until it's finished. Wash it down with the Living Water. We want to be just like Jesus, so at the end of our lives, we can say, "It is finished." God's will and our willingness to obey Him are inseparable, much like cake and ice cream! This truly is our "slice of life!"

## Drink the Living Water

"For the Father loves the Son and shows him all he does. Yes, to your amazement he will show him even greater things than these. For just as the Father raises the dead and gives them life, even so the Son gives life to whom is pleased to give it." [John 5:20-21]

"Jesus answered, 'I am the way and the truth and the life. No one comes to the Father except through me. If you really knew me, you would my Father as well. From now on, you do know him and have seen him.'" [John 14:6-7]

"The words I say to you are not just my own. Rather, it is the Father, living in me, who is doing his work. Believe me when I say that I am in the Father and the Father is in me; or at least believe on the evidence of the miracles themselves. I tell you the truth; anyone who has faith in me will do what I have been doing. He will do even greater things than these, because I am going to the Father. And I will do whatever you ask in my name, so that the Son may bring glory to the Father. You may ask me for anything in my name, and I will do it." [John 14: 10b-14]

"The thief comes only to steal and kill and destroy; I have come that they may have life, and have it to the full." [John 10:10]

"For I know the plans I have for you," declares the Lord, "plans to prosper you and not to harm you, plans to give you hope and a future." [Jeremiah 29:11]

## *Deeper Reflections*

— Okay, be honest, how many projects are you currently working on? Can you prioritize them? Are they all part of God's will for you at this point in your life? What might need to be left out if you are committed to excellence?

— Can you articulate God's will for your life, in general and specifically?

— What are the benefits of solitude in your life? What are the obstacles to finding times to be alone and quiet?

— Can you say that Jesus is your "slice of life," and that you are content with Him? Is He enough for you? Explain your answer.

## Drenched in Prayer

*To be honest, Lord, I admit that I get ahead of You sometimes, well...okay, many times! I need to be a better listener, so I can know Your will, not only for my future, but also my day—hour-by-hour and minute-by-minute. I have a long way to go, but I believe You will never leave me and You will see me through. When the enemy comes to steal, lie, or destroy the plans You have for me, please help me to stand my ground and never giving up the hope You died to give me. I look forward to the day we meet face to face in heaven, and I am so glad that nothing can separate me from Your love! Amen.*

# Field of Wheat

*Do you not say, "Four months more and then the harvest"? I tell you, open your eyes and look at the fields! They are ripe for harvest.* [ John 4:35 ]

After a long day at work, my husband and I like to take walks on the beautiful piece of property God has so graciously given us. During one of those walks, Tim showed me a field of wheat that a farmer he hired had planted on our twenty-one acres. It was gorgeous—all about the same height, golden brown, and blowing in the wind, like something you would imagine seeing in the movies. But then he told me, "It's time to cut it down."

I exclaimed, "But why? It's so pretty!"

He smiled and said, "That's why we planted it."

I understood, but was disappointed. About a month later, we took another walk, but this time that same field was filled with weeds. The wheat was an ugly brown, and it was no longer all the same height. I asked Tim, "Why haven't you harvested it?"

He replied, "I can't find a farmer to do it."

My husband is the greatest husband a girl could ever want, but a farmer he is not—a cowboy, maybe, but not a farmer!

I thought, "It's a shame to have planted all those seeds only to let the whole field go to waste. The longer the field goes without being harvested, the more the weeds overtake it." Tim has been calling every day for farmers to harvest the wheat, but he usually receives the same answer, "We're too busy," or "Your field just isn't large enough."

The more I thought about the wheat in this field, the more my heart broke. The only way I can figure out how to harvest this field is to cut it down myself—stalk by stalk. Before you think I'm some lunatic or something, be assured that I don't plan to do that! But I believe God never wastes a thing, and all things work to our good when we love Him. He used this experience to teach me a valuable lesson.

I believe God has sent us, the Women at His Well, a message today. He wants to tell us, "The way to harvest in this busy, self-centered world is one person at a time. Don't worry about what is in it for you, and don't become discouraged if you don't get to every person. Don't make excuses. Just look around you and see who I have put in your path. If you don't act soon, evil will spread. But take heart, for I have overcome the world. Look beyond what you see, think eternally, and persevere in My Power."

Our Heavenly Father amazes me with His ability to take a field of wheat that looked like a hopeless disaster, and still use it to motivate us to take action to reach people. He never wastes a thing, and He's still our Redeemer! What a joy it is to work in His field, doing His will. That is my spiritual nourishment for today. What's yours?

Jesus tells us to open our eyes and look at the fields! They are ripe for harvest today.

## Drink the Living Water

"Then he said to his disciples, 'The harvest is plentiful but the workers are few. Ask the Lord of the harvest, therefore, to send out workers into his harvest field.'" [Matthew 9:37]

"Then he left the crowd and went into the house. His disciples came to him and said, 'Explain to us the parable of the weeds in the field.' He answered, 'The one who sowed the good seed is the Son of Man. The field is the world, and the good seed stands for the sons of the kingdom. The weeds are the sons of the evil one, and the enemy who sows them is the devil. The harvest is the end of the age, and the harvesters are angels. As the weeds are pulled up and burned in the fire, so it will be at the end of the age. The Son of Man will send out his angels, and they will weed out of his kingdom everything that causes sin and all who do evil. They will throw them into the fiery furnace, where there will be weeping and gnashing of teeth. Then the righteous will shine like the sun in the kingdom of the Father. He who has ears, let him hear.'" [Matthew 13:36-43]

"Swing the sickle, for the harvest is ripe. Come, trample the grapes, for the winepress is full and the vats overflow—so great is their wickedness! Multitudes, multitudes in the valley of decision! For the day of the Lord is near in the valley of decision." [Joel 3:13-14]

## *Deeper Reflections*

— When is the last time you took a walk, either by yourself or with a friend or family member to admire God's creation? Describe a time when God taught you a lesson as you observed the natural world.

— What would you say is your own wheat field in God's harvest?

— What do you need in order to be an effective worker in His field?

— What will be your reward?

## Drenched in Prayer

*Lord of the Harvest, I pray that You will send more workers out into Your fields today. Prepare them, provide for them, send them and reward them with Your spiritual blessings. And Lord, send me. Amen.*

# Sowing and Reaping

*Thus the saying "One sows and another reaps" is true.* [ John 4:37 ]

Jesus taught us that storytelling is a great way to get His truths across, so let me share another personal story with you today.

One day after a *long* speaking engagement, I found myself sitting alone, tired, and exhausted at the Atlanta Airport awaiting my flight to Dayton, Ohio. I was devouring a chicken salad sandwich (I tend to get very hungry after speaking), when the Holy Spirit nudged me to get my attention. I sensed Him saying to me, "That young woman over there needs your help." My eyes gazed up to find a mother with two little boys sitting across from me. She seemed to be very distressed. I wondered, "Was she on drugs, hung-over, extremely sick, or escaping an abusive husband? Or maybe she was homeless and in the airport trying to stay warm." My mind reeled, and I wondered what might be required of me if I accepted this mission. I could see myself coming home after three days away with three extra houseguests, "Hi honey, I'm home!" And I thought about the possibility of emptying my purse to give her money for food. So many ideas…I decided to finish my chicken salad instead.

Suddenly, my spirit was screaming: "Don't miss this!"

When I looked up, she was gone. I was devastated. I knew I was the one who lost out, and I knew I had been selfish and disobedient. I was tired, but that was no excuse. I prayed, "Lord, please bring her back, otherwise I'll just pray for her." I looked up from my prayer, and there she was, sitting on the floor with her boys. Never have I catapulted so fast out of a seat to the floor beside someone!

As I looked into her eyes, I decided this wasn't the time for small talk, so I got right to the point, "God told me you needed help. What can I do for you?"

Her response floored me (pardon the pun). She looked at me and said, "My husband is a missionary in Africa. I'm flying home, but I'm extremely sick from the turbulence on the last flight."

Whew! That's not at all what I expected! I asked, "Where are you traveling to?"

"Dayton, Ohio," she barely whispered.

I smiled, thinking to myself, "Well, now I have the flight plan straight from God!"

I asked if I could pray for her. As I sat on the floor of the Atlanta Airport with three strangers, holding the tiny fingers of the children and praying for their mommy, God was working. I was sowing, and she was reaping, but wait….

As God would have it, our seat assignments were under His divine control. Yes, you guessed it. We were all in the same row. I was able to help care for the darling children who told me ever so openly and with childlike faith, "Our daddy tells people about Jesus!" To entertain them, I gave them some stickers that I had stuck in my book before I left home. Why I put them there, I would never have known....

About half way through the flight, the young woman finally began to *smile*. "I feel so much better. Thank you," she exclaimed.

"Praise the Lord!" was my outward response as I inwardly was thanking God for the second chance to follow His leading.

After that adventure, I felt refreshed. Truly, doing His will gave me spiritual refreshment I needed to get me through that day. I tell you, sowing can be just as rewarding and just as remarkable as the reaping. Did I sow or did I reap that day? I don't know, but I know that God is good. When we apply His Word, we find great joy in serving Him and in being obedient to His nudges.

Chicken salad will never taste the same!

## *Drink the Living Water*

"Sow for yourselves righteousness, reap the fruit of unfailing love, and break up your unplowed ground; for it is time to seek the Lord, until he comes and showers righteousness on you." [Hosea 10:12]

"Remember this: Whoever sows sparingly will also reap sparingly, and whoever sows generously will also reap generously. Each man should give what he has decided in his heart to give, not reluctantly or under compulsion, for God loves a cheerful giver. And God is able to make all grace abound to you, so that in all things at all times, having all that you need, you will abound in every good work. As it is written: 'He has scattered abroad his gifts to the poor; his righteousness endures forever.' Now he who supplies seed to the sower and bread for food will also supply and increase your store of seed and will enlarge the harvest of your righteousness. You will be made rich in every way so that you can be generous on every occasion, and through us your generosity will result in thanksgiving to God." [2 Corinthians 9:6-12]

"Then he told them many things in parables, saying: 'A farmer went out to sow his seed. As he was scattering the seed, some fell along the path, and the birds came and ate it up. Some fell on rocky places, where it did not have much soil. It sprang up quickly because the soil was shallow. But when the sun came up, the plants were scorched, and they withered because they had no root. Other seed fell among thorns, which grew up and choked the plants. Still other seed fell on good soil, where it produced a crop—a hundred, sixty or thirty times what was sown. He who has ears, let him hear.'" [Matthew 13:3-9

## *Deeper Reflections*

— Think about the past 24 hours in your life. What have you sown? Kind words, encouragement, prayer, or perhaps ugly words, complaints, and criticism? Write an inventory of the seeds you have sown and in whose lives you have sown them.

— Think of two or three of these seeds you have sown, and identify what you have reaped in return.

— What are some of the blessings you have reaped from God's Word sown into your heart?

## Drenched in Prayer

*Lord, I have reaped such a wonderful benefit from Your gift of eternal life. Your extravagant, boundless love is the best blessing I could ever ask for or imagine. And I know that You desire to continue giving good gifts to me, Your daughter, a Woman of the Well. Show me how to sow good seed in Your fields today. Help me to speak words of life and blessing to everyone I meet. In Jesus Name, I pray. Amen.*

# *Kingdom Building*

*I sent you to reap what you have not worked for. Others have done the hard work, and you have reaped the benefits of their labor.*

[ John 4:38 ]

Tim and I had the pleasure of building our "dream home," in 2001–2003. It was an incredibly spiritual adventure. Through the experience, God gave me insights into " building His Kingdom." Humor me today while I share some of those similarities with you—on the last leg of our journey together.

One of the first parallels is the *initial choice* "to build or not to build." The popular consensus is that building a house is almost always a disaster for the couple. Other comments include, "It's too much work, and not worth it," "I hope your marriage survives," or "Not me, baby!" Needless to say, for most people, building a house has negative connotations. Many people fear the complexity of the building process, or they're just too busy to consider it. Some believe it's a colossal waste of time.

I wonder if we respond to God's Kingdom building process much the same way? If offered the choice of eternal life in God's magnificent kingdom, how many of us say "Not me," assuming the worst, ignoring God's abundant love and forgiveness, or backing away in fear? If offered the chance to partner with God in the ministry of reconciliation, how many of us say, "Thanks, but it's too much trouble," or "I'd like to help, but I'm afraid others might think I'm weird or something."

As for me, I wouldn't have missed the chance to build our new home! What a growing and learning process! And yes, it had its share of ups and downs. In the same way, I don't want to miss a single minute of working with God on His Kingdom building. I've made the choice, and I'm not turning back. With that choice comes responsibility and some changes in priorities, but what an absolute privilege! Kingdom building, too, has its ups and downs, but I'm assured victory in the end. What *choice* have you made? If you are hesitant, what may be holding you back?

Another factor in building a house was the millions of *decisions* that must be made during the process. And each decision influences other choices. The selection of flooring affects the cabinet color, the cabinet color affects the countertops, and the countertops affect the faucet color. You get the idea!

I learned to enjoy each and every decision. And I learned to see all the choices from an overall perspective of budget, quality, resale, comfort, and functionality. Decisions were prayed over. How wonderful that we have a God who wants to be included and involved in every single decision and thought we have, right down to the tiniest of details! This insight has led to some reflection. If God is so in tune

with building my home, how much more must He care about the details of building His Kingdom? And if the individual elements of a
house affect each other, each part of the body of Christ must affect the
others, too. God is uniquely involved with every aspect of His family's
Kingdom building process, and He wants to be an "active builder"
who visits the job site each day! God is the ultimate Designer, Creator,
and Decision-Maker. Do you need to make a decision today regarding your service (or lack of it) in your role in Kingdom building? Our
choices have eternal implications.

Another similarity between house building and Kingdom building is the *time* involved. First, you select and purchase the property.
Then, you decide on the site of the home on that property. Next come
the architectural plans, the selection of a qualified builder, the choices
for each room, and then the actual construction of the home. Tim and
I have taken our time, so this has been a three-year process for us. If
we had rushed it, we would have made many mistakes along the way.
It could have been disastrous. (And at times, we came pretty close!)
Being sensitive to God's timing has given us the added gift of a great
mortgage rate!

God's timing is perfect—in building houses and in building His
Kingdom. We are His ministers; the builders of His Kingdom. He
has the blueprint and is totally qualified as our Architect. Each of us
plays a different part as we await the perfect timing of the construction
process. Our time is definitely in His hands. I have never been one for
patience, but the process of building a house has taught me that God's
gifts really are worth the wait.

The final parallel between building a house and building God's
Kingdom is in *moving in* and making it our home. I have to be honest
with you—this was the hardest part. Are you surprised? Everything

went quite well with the building process, but the day we moved in…
well, that's another story. Our moving company charged us double,
and then at five o'clock in the afternoon, our builder informed us we
would have no gas for the weekend. We had no hot water for showers,
and we weren't able to cook on the new, pretty, stainless cook top for
eleven miserable days. We were camping out in our new home! In fact,
the gas pipes eventually had to be removed and replaced.

This experience made me think of how uncomfortable we can be
when we accept the Lord Jesus into our hearts, yet we haven't really
let Him totally move in. Many years ago, Robert Boyd Munger wrote
a wonderful little book titled *My Heart—Christ's Home.* Munger observed that many of us invite Jesus into some rooms in our lives, but
we keep Him out of others. We keep some doors locked and bolted to
keep Him out, and we keep some of the utilities turned off! We may
be afraid that some things in those "rooms" of our lives need to be
replaced, let go of, or stopped, and we don't trust Him enough to let
Him have His way in those habits, relationships, or secret desires. We
have accepted His forgiveness, but we don't want any part of responsibility, accountability, or obedience.

There are plenty of responsibilities that require action on our part
in our new home. Our choices to keep the house up and running will
determine the quality of our lives while we live there. In the same
way, some of us still fail to understand the depth of God's love, and
we refuse to let Him have access to every room in our hearts. We may
still feel condemnation, guilt and shame, even though He has taken it
all away. We may have a new spirit, yet we are still living that dreadful
life of sin. We may know our purpose and plan in God's Kingdom, yet
we are still lackadaisical about walking in His Spirit and carrying out
His plan.

Moving in is the hardest part. As we open every part of our hearts to Christ and let Him go wherever He wants to go in our lives, we'll find that He transforms every part of us and makes us whole! As we keep our perspective eternal, and our eyes on the finish line, standing firm in our faith, we will receive a crown that outweighs them all. And we will hear those encouraging words, "Well done, good and faithful kingdom servant!"

Though I learned a lot in the building process, and I love my Kingdom building Boss, I look forward to joining Him in the room He has prepared especially for me in His dream home in Heaven! Until then, I want to be a faithful servant. I'm honored to be part of His building process, just like the Samaritan Woman!

The bottom line of our story today: When the Samaritan Woman began to help build God's Kingdom, it wasn't because her circumstances changed, it was because of the choices she made, the decision to follow Jesus, the time she spent with Him, and the fact that she allowed Him direct access to every room in her heart! The Holy Spirit now resided within her, and she believed!

## Drink the Living Water

"But as for me and my household, we will serve the Lord." [Joshua 25:15]

"All this is from God, who reconciled us to Himself through Christ and gave us the ministry of reconciliation; that God was reconciling the world to Himself in Christ, not counting men's sins against them." [2 Corinthians 5:18]

"Just as each of us has one body with many members, and the members do not all have the same function, so in Christ we who are many form one body, and each member belongs to all the others." [Romans 12:4]

"In my Father's house are many rooms; if it were not so, I would have told you. I am going there to prepare a place for you." [John 14:2]

"Surely goodness and love will follow me all the days of my life, and I will dwell in the house of the Lord forever." [Psalm 23:6]

## Deeper Reflections

— As you think back over the lessons in this book, what are the two or three most important insights you've learned?

— In your study and reflection, have you grown in ways that surprise you? Explain your answer.

— In what ways has your concept of God's goodness and grace been strengthened?

— Write a thank you note to the Lord for the ways He met you during this study. Be specific.

— What's the next step for you (another Bible study, a devotional, a book of the Bible to study in depth, etc.)?

## Drenched in Prayer

*Jesus, thank You for meeting me, a ragged, tired woman at the Gushing Spring of Your grace and mercy. How can I ever thank You enough for the life You have given freely to me? Help me to live each day as if it were my last, to cherish each moment, to pour out the love and forgiveness to others that You have poured out on me. Words are just not enough to express my thanks for all the times You met me right where I was during this study. You are just incredible, and Your timing is perfect. You are my Messiah, I believe in You, I believe You died to save me and the only way to Eternal Life is through You. I accept You now into my heart, and pray that You will pour out Your Spirit on me. I also accept the challenge to go in peace to love and serve You, my Lord, my Savior, and my Redeemer. In the beautiful, sweet name of Jesus. Amen.*

# Revelation
# Chapter 22

*Then the angel showed me the river of the water of life, as clear as crystal, flowing from the throne of God and of the Lamb down the middle of the great street of the city.* On each side of the river stood the tree of life, bearing twelve crops of fruit, yielding its fruit every month. And the leaves of the tree are for the healing of the nations. No longer will there be any curse. The throne of God and of the Lamb will be in the city, and his servants will serve him. They will see his face, and his name will be on their foreheads. There will be no more night. They will not need the light of a lamp or the light of the sun, for the Lord God will give them light. And they will reign forever and ever.

The angel said to me, "These words are trustworthy and true. The Lord, the God of the spirits of the prophets, sent his angel to show his servants the things that must soon take place."

"Behold, I am coming soon! Blessed is he who keeps the words of the prophecy in this book."

I, John, am the one who heard and saw these things. And when I had heard and seen them, I fell down to worship at the feet of the angel who had been showing them to me. But he said to me, 'Do not do it! I am a fellow servant with you and with your brothers the prophets and of all who keep the words of this book. Worship God!"

Then he told me, "Do not seal up the words of the prophecy of this book, because the time is near. Let him who does wrong continue to do wrong; let him who is vile continue to be vile; let him who does right continue to do right; and let him who is holy continue to be holy."

"Behold, I am coming soon! My reward is with me, and I will give to everyone according to what he has done. I am the Alpha and the Omega, the First and the Last, the Beginning and the End."

"Blessed are those who wash their robes, that they may have the right to the tree of life and may go through the gates into the city. Outside are the dogs, those who practice magic arts, the sexually immoral, the murderers, the idolaters and everyone who loves and practices falsehood.

"I, Jesus, have sent my angel to give you this testimony for the churches. I am the Root and the Offspring of David, and the bright Morning Star."

The Spirit and the bride say, "Come! And let him who hears say, "Come!" *Whoever is thirsty, let him come; and whoever wishes, let him take the free gift of the water of life.*

I warn everyone who hears the words of the prophecy of this book: If anyone adds anything to them, God will add to him the plagues described in this book. And if anyone takes words away from this book of prophecy, God will take away from him his share in the tree of life and in the holy city, which are described in this book.

He who testifies to these things says, "Yes, I am coming soon." Amen. Come, Lord Jesus.

The grace of the Lord Jesus be with God's people. Amen.

# Epilogue

Dear Well Dwellers,

Have you ever considered that *you* are actually God's arms? Isaiah 51:9 says, "Awake, awake! Clothe yourself with strength, O arm of the Lord." What an exciting thought! I picture your arms folded in prayer to Him right now. He says in Isaiah that our strength is found in quietness and confidence, rest and repentance. As Women of the Well, we must be quiet before Him so we can walk in the confidence of His promises. These promises bring us the strength we need to face our many challenges each day.

I trust that God has kindled a fire in your heart through the power of His Holy Spirit. Now we both can be His arms to kindle that same fire to others.

I was once like that Woman at the Well. (I occasionally give my testimony in speaking engagements, if you are interested look up my schedule, to see when I am near you! We need to meet!) In the gospel story, she began with no hope and no purpose, yet God graciously used her to transform the lives of many in Samaria. It began with her, the one person who needed Jesus the most. He changed her and He has changed me, and He continues to mold me every day! After all, I'm just a vessel of clay.

Has Jesus changed your life? If so, there's power in your testimony that you may never have realized up to this point. When we drink of the Well of Living Water, we need to learn from the Samaritan Woman and pour out what we take in. Otherwise, we risk becoming dried up prunes... I mean wells!

God's salvation never dries up—it lasts forever. Do you know anyone or anything that lasts forever? No, everything rusts, fades, and disintegrates, but God's salvation lasts for all of eternity. What a wonderful gift He has given us!

My very favorite verse of all time is…drum roll please…Isaiah 12:3 "With joy you will draw water from the wells of salvation." It's impossible to draw water from the wells of salvation without joy! And who doesn't need joy these days? It's also impossible to draw physical water from a well without arms! We are God's spiritual arms to a hurting world, as we ourselves dive into His spiritual Well of Living Water.

So I'm wondering, has the message God gave me for you over the last 35 days made a difference in your life? I assure you, it isn't my message. It's God's.

This, then, is the point I want to make: We are God's messengers, His arms to the world. The city or town where each of us lives has some thirsty souls that need our arms to pour God's water of salvation out to them. Psalm 116:13 tells us, "I will lift up God's cup of salvation." Jesus certainly poured out His blood for our salvation.

A person that is mighty in the Spirit listens to God and is willing to obey Him. The question is: Am I willing? Are you? Will you join Women of the Well in pouring the Living Water out to people around you? Will you awake and come with us? Will you be God's arms? I'm not asking that you be completely free from fear and doubt. We all experience these from time to time. But God's great love casts our fear and His truth dispels doubt. Be honest about any hesitant thoughts, and take them to the throne of grace. By golly, do it afraid!

I hope we can minister together in God's Spirit and bring this flicker to a flame! My arms are folded in prayer as God continues to speak to all our hearts. Please take time to go to His Well and listen, and if you hear His voice calling you, be obedient to His call. You may even want to write me with your own Woman of the Well story for a future book! And remember:

As *Women of the Well,* we are:

- *Well-advised* as we are drenched in wisdom by the Holy Spirit,
- *Well-appointed* by the King who chose us as His special treasures,
- *Well-born* into the family of the highest position to God our Father,
- *Well-bred* due to our spiritual reparenting,
- *Well-fed* by Him who promises to meet all our needs,
- *Well-formed* as God knitted us together in our mother's womb,
- *Well-preserved* because of our eternal life in Christ,
- *Well-read* as we develop a thirst for His Word daily,
- *Well-off* as we learn to live life victoriously, and
- *Well-to-do* because of our inheritance in Him!

But we are *not* empty well-wishers, nor are we wishy-washy, wimpy wallops (I made that one up!) or second guessers! We claim our rights in Christ at the Well of Living Water. We pray in faith the prayers of a warrior, not because of anything we have done, but because we have victory through Christ at the cross. Amen!

I want to end with this analogy: Think of your favorite war movie. (Okay, think hard!) Play it all the way through. You know who the victor of the battle is. Now think more about the hardest, most perilous part of the battle. That's where we are in our spiritual battle. We're in the *heat* of the battle, but because we drink daily from the Victor's Well of salvation, we can fight with renewed confidence. We're convinced we're on the winning team. Our battle is not against flesh and blood; it's a spiritual fight. We live not in time, but in eternity! The enemy is out to destroy our faith and prevent us from visiting the Well, but we resist him and drink deeply. Are you winning the battle at this point in your life?

Jesus Christ is the Living Water of our well-tended souls. It's the Women of the Well's mission to help women make God their top priority, see life from Jesus' perspective and experience the overflowing power of the Holy Spirit.

The choice is ours. To be *well* means to be restored, to be whole. That's what God wants for you and me.

I love each of you, and I have truly enjoyed our time together! It has been a privilege. Thanks for joining me! May it be well with your soul as you continue drinking from the *Gushing Springs* of His Love. All Glory to God!

*Drenched in His Extravagant Grace,*
*Deborah*

# A Plan for Salvation—
# Eternal Life in Heaven

"For all have sinned and fall short of the glory of God." [Romans 3:23]

Admit that you are a sinner.

"But God demonstrates His own love for us in this; While we were still sinners, Christ died for us." [Romans 5:8]

Acknowledge that Christ died for you personally.

"The wages of sin is death, but the gift of God is eternal life in Christ Jesus our Lord." [Romans 6:23]

Accept the free gift.

"That if you confess with your mouth, 'Jesus is Lord,' and believe in your heart that God raised Him from the dead, you shall be saved. For it is with your heart that you believe and are justified, and it is with your mouth that you confess and are saved." [Romans 10:9-10]

Agree by submitting your life to God and believing Him and His Word.

"And you also were included in Christ when you heard the word of truth, the gospel of your salvation. Having believed, you were marked in him with a seal, the promised Holy Spirit, who is a deposit guaranteeing our inheritance until the redemption of those who are God's possession—to the praise of his glory." [Ephesians 1:13-14]

## *Pray:*

*Lord I am a sinner and fall short of your glory. I believe Jesus died for me personally and desires to have a personal relationship with me. I know that to not be reborn spiritually will result in a spiritual death, but I have decided to follow Jesus and be accepted through faith into the Kingdom of God and to have eternal life with Jesus through grace. I believe from this moment forward, I have been given the Holy Spirit as a sign of my inheritance, and I have been sealed by Him for redemption of my sins. I love you Lord, take over my life, my heart, my body, my emotions and my spirit. Amen.*

If you prayed this prayer to receive Jesus gift of eternal life please contact your local Women's ministry leader or Pastor at a church near you. Also drop me a note, so I can celebrate for you! Did you know that for every sinner that repents, the angels in heaven throw a party? I have always been a party waiting to happen, so I would love to share in your excitement! God bless you!

# About
# Women of the Well Ministry

Women of the Well Ministry was founded by Deborah Lovett, a motivational speaker who teaches creatively. She inspires women from all walks of life and appeals to women of all ages. Her flair for style, humor, and personal anecdotes, combined with her stimulating presentation of godly wisdom, will leave women bathing in God's fountain of faith, hope and love! Her speaking style has been noted as "open, genuine, and soothing."

Ladies will feel refreshed and invigorated, as if they had personally met Jesus, just like the Samaritan Woman did at the well so many years ago. Peace, harmony, contentment, clarity of mind, and a new or renewed joy for Christ are the end result of spending an afternoon or evening with Deborah, as she draws from the well of "Living Water" and quenches the thirst of women everywhere.

How did WOW get its name? Deborah named her ministry after God told her, "Deb, it's high time women did more than just come up to the Well for a dip or two. They need to dive in and take a bath in it!" Deb understood God's intent that we are to be Women of the Well and not women of the world. For this reason, Deb is intentional about her morning and evening quiet times with Jesus, which she refers to as her "daily trips to the Well."

Women of the Well's mission is to motivate and teach women how to make God their top priority, see life from Jesus' perspective, and to walk in the overflowing power of the Holy Spirit.

WOW offers a special "IT IS WELL WITH MY SOUL AD-VANCE" for Women's Groups which includes a three session workshop:

- Session One: The Woman and The Water (by Deborah Lovett)
- Session Two: The Worship and The Witness (by Deborah Lovett)
- Session Three: The Warfare and The Warrior (by Nona Anderson, speaker and contributing writer for Women of the Well)

Options are available for one, two, or three of the sessions.

Contact Deborah for information regarding this ADVANCE or other speaking opportunities: 1-937-609-5015.

"Weekend Water from the Well" is a free motivational that comes directly to your email address on Saturday and/or Sunday. It is written by one of several contributing writers for Women of the Well, including Deborah. This devotional is based on the true and inspiring Word of God. To sign up or for more information regarding Women of the Well ministry visit: www.womenofthewell.org

Women of the Well is a non-profit organization.

# About the Author

Deborah Lovett's main credential is her great love for Jesus (Luke 7:47). She was the Women's Ministry Director at her local church, as well as a Sunday School teacher for women. In the past, Deb chaired the Christian Women's Club of South Dayton, Ohio. She is also a graduate of CLASS (Christian Leaders Authors and Speakers Services). She is an entrepreneur for Jesus, and she makes herself available before or after any speaking engagement for consultation on launching a Women's Ministry Program or Discipleship/Mentoring Program.

Deb and her husband Tim live in Ohio and have been married seventeen years. The Lovett family has two children, a creative daughter and a humorous son—which makes for memorable occasions on a daily basis!

# Here's what leaders are saying about Deborah Lovett:

"Deborah's faith is contagious. When you sit across the table from her, you can't help but notice her passion for the heart of God. When she thinks of other women discovering His heart, she is driven to reach out even more through her speaking, writing, and mentoring. If ever our hurting world needed a teacher who leads us easily to the heart of the Father, Deborah is it! I delight in being her friend."
—*Christine Wyrtzen, Founder of Daughters of Promise*

"Deborah has the ability to captivate her audience with her unique style of teaching. She builds curiosity as she unfolds a message of deep meaningful truth from the Word of God. Deborah's delightful sense of humor coupled with her sincere desire to reveal the loving heart of God is an experience any woman would love to encounter!"
—*Rose Britner, Founder, Women of Grace Ministries*

"In her desire to sit at the feet of Jesus and learn of Him, Deb Lovett reminds me of Mary, the sister of Martha. Deb's devotion to the Lord and focus on her family expresses for me the passion and perseverance of Hannah, the mother of Samuel. Her gentle approach in serving and ministering to others is a reflection of the lowly spirit of Mary, the mother of our Lord. Her ministry with WOW is a vibrant fulfillment of her goal and mission to glorify Christ and to build up His church. Deb is a faithful and involved member in her local church. I fully endorse and commend her as one who will minister with excellence, effectiveness, and enthusiasm."
—*Dr. Kenneth Liu, Board of Directors, The Christian Missionary Alliance and Senior Pastor of Centerville Community Church*

"What I appreciated most about Deborah's ministry to the women of our church was not only to give the message, but to make true followers--disciples who live out that calling. By having her come to our church to speak, I gained a friend. You will too."
—*Cindy Zimmerman, Pastor's Wife*

"Not long ago, my children asked me, *Mom, if you could be like anyone in the world, who would it be?* Without missing a beat, I said, 'Mrs. Lovett.' My admiration for Deb has nothing to do with her extraordinary gift as a Bible teacher. I admire her because of who she is in her own home and how she conducts her personal life. Deb is madly in love with Jesus. It's that simple. And the more time you spend with her, up-close and personal, the more you discover how passionate she is about her Lord. I've toured with many of America's leading Christian communicators, but I've never met anyone with a deeper, more authentic relationship with God than Deb Lovett."
—*Donna Partow, Author of* Becoming a Vessel God Can Use and Becoming the Woman I Want to Be

# To Order More Copies

*Gushing Springs* is designed to be used by individuals and groups. The reflection questions at the end of each day's lesson stimulate application of Biblical truth, and they work very well to foster discussions in small groups.

Books are $15.00 each, and shipping and handling is $3.00 each.

To order, send a check or money order to:
    Women of the Well Ministry
    P.O. Box 367
    Bellbrook, Ohio 45305

For orders in excess of ten books, the price is $13.00 each, and $2.00 shipping and handling for each book.

Check the website for special offers, discounts, and other available items. Go to: **www.womenofthewell.org**